The Economy of One

*Creating Opportunity
Instead of Chasing Jobs*

Program Participant Workbook

By

Elizabeth Allen

&

Frank Bonura

ISBN-13: 978-1983875595

ISBN-10: 1983875597

Contents

Introduction

Overview

This program teaches The Economy of One methodology. The goal is to train participants in an entirely different way of managing and thinking about their careers and themselves in our new era of outsourcing and expendability.

The program breaks down the process into a series of doable steps that will address your attitude, skillsets and behaviors that are required to engage. Unlike traditional HR transition assistance and jobseeker programs, this program focuses on training participants to create opportunities versus "just chasing jobs" by systematically managing relationships for the purpose of creating mutual value, true opportunities and revenue. It's a market-proven approach, broken down into workable steps for the average person who struggles with how to engage when transition is required.

For people in a professional slump, this approach provides tools—emotional, relational and practical tools—to reignite otherwise stagnant careers. Others who are enjoying a measure of professional success will find that they are already doing intuitively many of the steps that The Economy of One teaches. The difference is, now they will learn to do them systematically, with clear tasks, templates, deadlines and accountability.

The Economy of One program produces measurable economic benefit to people who put it into practice. Why is this important? It's important because people need innovative options that offset economic uncertainty by producing multiple streams of reliable income. The goal of this program is to provide a method that empowers you to never be at the mercy of HR, job boards or without a pipeline of opportunities ever again. Ultimately, The Economy of One gives participants hope and the practical help that is required to take control of their life's direction.

Course Content

This program runs for ten modules. We've put the concepts into video presentations on YouTube, but also have included this Participant guide to review key ideas and written exercises in detail. In our video series, and on our website (EconomyOfOne.com), there are additional tools and templates, FAQ's for each module, as well as definitions of key terms you will see used in each module. Sign up for our newsletter from our website and get regular tips on the program. Whether you are taking this online or offline, we suggest participants either attend a minimum of ten offline group meetings (one for each module) or self-pace through the video presentations with the intention to join a weekly accountability group offline or online. The Economy of One focuses on personal accountability, coaching and support. The accountability group assists with your transition to applying concepts associated with this process.

- Module One: Introduction—Creating Opportunities vs. Chasing Jobs
- Module Two: The Story Of You
- Module Three: Relationships vs. Networks
- Module Four: Creating Personal And Professional Opportunities
- Module Five: Start With Your MAP
- Module Six: The YBR
- Module Seven: Leaving A Good Footprint
- Module Eight: Negotiate Compensation And Close
- Module Nine: On-boarding
- Module Ten: Welcome To A New Way Of Life

Target Audience

For whom is this course designed? This program is designed for anyone who is in transition, either from the loss of a job, transition from an existing job or out of concern for losing one. Additionally, this course is designed for any individuals with a desire to explore other career options or entrepreneurship. It includes people who are interested in creating diverse income streams for their family or those desiring to improve their outcomes in professional relationships and career management. Specific groups include Military personnel transitioning to civilian work, underemployed Millennials, mid-or senior level managers who are being squeezed out of employment, people exploring entrepreneurship or working as independent contractors, and older workers struggling in the job market due to outdated or underappreciated skillsets.

What You Will Learn

Use a step-by-step process to effectively identify and explore all of your options. Looking for full-time employment is just one of many available paths. You will learn to uncover options that are not so obvious. These include things like stopgap solutions to create income during the wider opportunity hunt, and volunteer opportunities that increase your skills, build relationships, expand the warehouse of talents while increasing overall marketability. You will find your thinking challenged and find comfort in the data and facts that illustrate "why the system isn't working." You will be encouraged and empowered to make the paradigm shift required to more effectively build relationships that open the door to sincere opportunity.

Strategically communicate, self-promote and network. THE ECONOMY OF ONE's simple, doable steps will take the guesswork out of where to begin and how to make measurable progress. You will explore the roles and responsibilities critical to seeing measurable progress, and gain tools (mindsets, skills and behaviors) required to radically organize and accelerate your efforts. We will also address various mental barriers to success and provide troubleshooting exercises to help you move safely out of your comfort zones.

Recapture confidence. You will learn a specific process designed to guide and empower you throughout the relationship building job hunt, or opportunity identification process. The processes will help you evaluate your level of interest in each new opportunity, give you tools to objectively compare possibilities, and empower you to follow strategic direction as you interact with potential employers and build relationships that can result in true opportunity as opposed to "just a job."

Capitalize on insight into the mindset of hiring managers. Since three out of four opportunities are offered by small to mid-size companies, it is essential to understand the company's priorities *before* interviewing with such employers. You will learn about the intuitive thinking and behavior of entrepreneurs, as well as the roles and skillsets they value. And you also will learn how to address the "unspoken agenda" of each interaction—an agenda that most jobseekers are completely unaware of.

Create and use a custom MAP of relationships. THE ECONOMY OF ONE will guide you through creating a Marketing Action Plan (MAP™) that includes your relationships—both real and desired. This plan will guide your efforts over the next 6-12 months, and then onward throughout your career. The MAP will act as both a compass and a measure of your overall social contributions and influence. While the MAP's primary function is to connect to opportunities through people, it also will give you a renewed sense of purpose and meaning as the goal is to provide mutual value to others in every interaction (taking the focus off "what's in it for me").

Use accountability to enhance results. You will find and develop a relationship with accountability partners who will keep you on track with measurable goals, deadlines and feedback. These partners or small groups will encourage each other to step outside of personal comfort zones relationally, developing skills that will help to reveal the opportunities you really want (instead of retrofitting yourself into some abstract job description that isn't what you want).

Objectively monitor progress to improve their results. You will learn how to approach every networking event, job fair, and interview with a relationally focused plan. You will also learn how to proactively qualify the value of relationships to create employment or opportunities in a timely manner.

Achieve transparency. Most people are not completely alone in their situation and have significant others depending on them. Recognizing this, we have provided a way through THE ECONOMY OF ONE for you to communicate to others the progress you have objectively made. This makes conversations that start with, "How's the job search going?" more fruitful as you are now equipped to provide concrete answers and receive more targeted encouragement.

Turn encouragement and constructive feedback into measurable growth. This course will re-energize you and jumpstart your efforts. Facilitators will cultivate a supportive environment while at the same time challenging you with a new framework of thinking. Our goal is to deliver extraordinary encouragement (and hope) along with the tools (help) to bring success into reality.

Reconnect to passion, proficiency and productivity. You will identify the options that are best suited for your natural abilities, interests and experience. Our goal is that you will never be without options, income, or opportunities again. We will make sure that you are no longer at the mercy of job boards, recruiters, headhunters, and HR departments. We will empower you to find yourself in firm control of your destiny by following a clear plan and exact process by which to engage.

Before you begin…We need to tell you that this program is designed to dramatically change and impact your understandings of the job search and value creation (development of income stream options) process. It will radically redefine your notion of what a job is and cause you to ask, "what am I really looking for?" If you are someone who has worked your entire career, or to this point for a paycheck and you are living paycheck to paycheck, we understand. We want to say upfront that this course might not be a fit for you as you may be simply looking for a way to keep the lights on and pay your bills. We are not assuming this about you, but we are acknowledging that this may be a possibility as what might be motivating you is a need for a paycheck. If this is the case, this course may <u>not</u> be for you because we are going to redefine your options for a future filled with hope for meaningful work. This being our goal, we must disclose upfront that it will require you to think and behave very differently. Are you ready to do this? Are you *committed* to doing this?

In this process we are also going to teach you in three different ways. We will teach through this workbook, through our online video series, and through your small group interactions. The workbook is designed to introduce key concepts and ideas, explaining to you <u>what to do and how to do it</u>. The video series is different. It features the authors sharing with you greater detail on our experiences that will frame up the psychology of <u>why </u>this process works.

In the small accountability group that you will be asked to join, you will work on applying the process we present to your unique situation. You will do the exercises at the end of every module and set goals that monitor your progress moving forward. In this process of harnessing the power of accountability you will find new friends, better ways to think about things and the support you need to truly engage. We have found that this component of <u>accountability</u> is CRITICAL to creating forward momentum and sustainable changes to attitudes, skills, and behaviors. Why? Because part of creating new behaviors is letting go of behaviors and attitudes that do not work and hinder you in your ability to move forward. In an accountability group, you are not in an interview, so it is a safe place to explore what is working for you in positioning your value and what is not.

In the process of providing an entirely <u>new way</u> of looking at the challenges you face, we are going to use a lot of new words, terms, and phrases. We encourage you to be "okay" with this, and know that this a meaty course, full of new ideas and terms for you to grasp and apply. Since everyone has their own unique learning curve, do not be intimidated, but know that each module is packed with information and insights we hope you can immediately apply. All the words we use are defined in each module as well as in the Definitions of Terms section at the end of this workbook. Ready?

We are so excited to share with you genuinely good news in a world struggling with economic uncertainty….

Module One: Introduction—Creating Opportunity vs. Chasing Jobs

Objectives:

By the end of this module, you will know:

- The facts and supporting research that describes the employment marketplace, as well as the realities of key economic trends
- What is working and not working in the traditional HR driven processes, how to alter your perceptions, and thus your approach to "the process"
- What not to do (time wasters)
- What to do: how to break down your search for opportunity into doable steps
- Mindsets that must change for new attitudes, skillsets and behaviors to emerge that are required for measurable success
- Where we are headed in terms of the scope addressed by this course

Welcome to the New Normal!

Why are you here? *How do you feel about it?* For most, depending upon how long you have been in transition, there is some anxiety about the process. It is very natural to fear the unknown, as uncertainty is often expressed in very real financial and family concerns. Depending on where you are at in the process, you may be experiencing many different types of emotions. These emotions may include a myriad of feelings. Please take a moment to reflect upon, identify and note any feelings you might be having:

☐ Confident, but realize I should prepare or act now (time is on my side)
☐ Dread "the process"
☐ Baffled by the unknown, not sure where to start or what to expect
☐ Helpless, feeling at the mercy of traditional HR and job boards
☐ Resentful, sensing the process lacks dignity or mutual respect (I feel demeaned)
☐ Futile, I am sending out resumes without any results (limited to no response)
☐ Frustrated, that I cannot find anything that excites me (I do not like current options)
☐ Uncertain, I cannot rely on recruiters and headhunters
☐ Out of control, without a plan
☐ Powerless
☐ Depressed and anxious
☐ Anger, shame, or guilt about the circumstances surrounding this transition
☐ Alone, surrounded by people who may want to help, but aren't
☐ Helpless and / or hopeless
☐ Stuck

- **Why reflect on how you feel?** Because how you feel today is important to predicting how you will behave tomorrow (at interviews and in interactions with others.) What do we mean by this? We have observed that many people in transition have *unresolved emotions* about the experience. It may be anger at the reason they were terminated, it may be a feeling of shock or disbelief that this is even happening to them, it may be shame or a sense of abandonment by those they trusted (friends who they thought would help them, who now turn a cold shoulder). It may be a sense of bewilderment at a process you have not anticipated and feel no control over. No matter what the scope of emotions you are feeling, we encourage you to simply begin the process of identifying where you are at by reflecting on the list presented above. However you feel, know it is perfectly normal (we see it all the time), and it is okay to start from this place.

- **How do you move forward?** We will assign you to join a small group of peers who are also going through the transition process. We call this an "accountability group" because it is a safe place to get real about your feelings about the process. It is a group where you can give voice to your feelings without being judged, yet you will be lovingly encouraged to work through the emotions so that you can let them go in order to move forward. We have found that when you feel you've lost your identity; you can regain your sense of authenticity and purpose by connecting with others in a safe place designed to address the issues. When people unite for this purpose, everyone focuses on listening, being objective, and offering insight to identify toxic attitudes or behaviors, that if not dealt with, tend to surface in interviews or key interactions with others. This type of support, when combined with a highly structured process, provides people exact steps in which to meaningfully engage. We will talk more about this in later modules, but for now, know we will sincerely assist with this process and have designed specific tools and tested processes to help you.

Here's Good News...

We are going to provide a highly proven (yet unorthodox) method that can change your perceptions and directly impact your outcomes. We will do this by first challenging your thinking, and second by changing your behavior, providing exact steps you need to do while in transition. Why do a different process? Simply, the traditional HR systems we are relying upon are broken. *They are not working.* This is evidenced by the millions of talented workers who are discouraged and have officially "stopped looking" for work. It is also evidenced by people who are genuinely skilled and are seemingly not able to "find work."

Why is this happening? Companies have taken a process that is quite simple and have made it *far too complex*. Stop and think about this for a moment. Before the printing press, how were people hired? Someone would hear about a person's skills via a <u>relationship,</u> and then the reputation of the person, in conjunction with the quality of their work, would lead the individual to be offered a job or opportunity. Pretty simple. Today, companies have made this otherwise simple process far too complicated. How? Legal advisors and HR have combined forces to protect the interests of companies in such a way that they have actually designed a process that is perfect for screening out the candidates and talent that they hope to hire and attract!

Key word searches that are applied by HR to identify perfect candidates are functioning to screen out very good applicants. How? Applicants are told they should incorporate key words on what is otherwise meaningless documentation (resumes that do not describe how you will use your primary talents to do the work and do it profitably for the company). The result is that hundreds of candidates are generated, one of which cannot be distinguished from another because they are all saying essentially the exact same thing! All candidates appear similar (due to key words) and consequently, HR finds itself sorting through piles of paper that mean little to nothing in terms of quality and "right fit." HR chokes under the weight of its own inefficiency, and the quality candidate rarely connects with the right opportunity (we define "right opportunity" as something that is a great fit for you personally and is profitable for those that depend on you). People are discouraged and disengage over time from lack of response. Companies lament the process claiming that there's "no talent." Technology designed to help the situation has hurt it, and the process is "broken."

Marketplace Myths

What is equally disturbing is that this broken HR process has fostered myths in the marketplace that truly damage the psyche and mindset of the person facing transition. *What myths you ask?* Here is the dirty dozen. Read the following and ask yourself how frequently you have encountered these conclusions as described by the media, perhaps so much that you too now *actually believe* them...

- ☐ Resumes represent meaningful documentation
- ☐ There is a talent shortage
- ☐ Traditional HR understands the work that needs to be done
- ☐ HR does the hiring
- ☐ Job descriptions tell the whole story
- ☐ The primary reason people are hired is because they are talented
- ☐ Retrofitting who you are as a person for a paycheck is satisfying
- ☐ Job boards are a viable route to opportunity
- ☐ Real offers are based on your last salary, a W2, or someone else's salary survey
- ☐ Your ability to create value and impact is determined by age
- ☐ Behavioral interviews have meaning
- ☐ Networking, connections and relationships are all the same thing

If you are dismayed by this list, be assured that we will address each of these myths, providing evidence to support our conclusions that will help rewire and reposition your thinking.

A Job Versus An Opportunity

If these myths are familiar, it is because these notions are core to how people tend to think about the job seeking and transition process. We want to address head on that if you need a paycheck to cover your bills, then there's no shame in pursuing a "job." Definitely get a job to feed your family and meet your basic financial needs. However, we believe that based on years of experience that most people are not looking for another "job." They are instead looking for a real opportunity, but simply have not known how to go about identifying and generating what will be a good fit for them. We define an opportunity as something that *genuinely* excites you, something that you want to "get up and do every day," something that is a good fit for you personally that genuinely meets the needs of your personal life and your family.

What's the key difference between a job and an opportunity? It all starts with you and your mindset of what you are willing to settle for. When you are seeking a job (defined by "a paycheck"), too often you begin behaving like a "desperate jobseeker." What *exactly* is a desperate jobseeker? It is someone who starts to feel powerless, who then begins to act powerless. They are being denied their human dignity as they are being driven to act subservient to a system that is demanding they set aside who they are in order to retrofit themselves into someone else's idea of "who they should be in order to get a job."

"Desperate Jobseekers"

The traditional process of seeking a job can feel like an act of human submission, which dehumanizes people by the very nature of the process and makes people feel "small." Behaviors of a desperate jobseeker include things like handing out your resume to everyone you know (who did not ask for it). You are asking them to determine "how you fit in" to anything they might know about. The results are that you provide a document that people then use to identify specific reasons *not* to consider you! Since you have provided a generic resume, you are not addressing the specific needs of the organization and are thus categorized as "unqualified." (*Next!*)

Other behaviors that contribute to the label of a "desperate jobseeker" include: succumbing to every request (having a subservient attitude), re-engineering yourself to fit every situation or be hirable by everybody, compromising who you are as a person and what you want professionally in order to focus on a paycheck. This may result in compromising your values to work for a less than honorable company because you must have a paycheck. Many people we work with have said "I'm not a desperate jobseeker" and yet, *they act like one* through these self-defeating behaviors and mindsets we have described. One objective we have in this course is to make you aware of attitudes and behaviors that reinforce the *perception of desperate jobseeker* so that you can avoid this pitfall. If you struggle to re-frame your mindset, do not feel alone. When you examine the facts supporting today's transitional marketplace, it is easy to see where a desperate mindset might come from.

Do not worry about how you will explain these new concepts to other people that might be approaching the transitional challenge with you (your family or significant other). We understand that it may not be "just you" making decisions in your household in terms of how to approach your transition. What we are advising you to do just might shock your spouse or significant other, so we suggest that they view Module One (or read this text) in order to understand the key ideas that seem to go against the grain of traditional advice you have encountered. As we provide details and options associated with your personal plan, it will provide comfort to those you might report progress to, but we would humbly ask that they too trust this process and learn with you to understand the reasons behind what we are advising. Also, recognize that it takes time to absorb the ideas, recalibrate your mindset and engage with activities that will result in opportunities. So, give yourself time to absorb and apply what you are about to engage in. Please include in the process those that have something at stake so that you will not create challenges at home. Your family will learn in parallel with your experience, which will make for a better experience for you overall.

Insights from twenty-year Army Veteran, COL Gregory Sharpe who successfully transitioned from the military to a desired new job in Bulgaria, where he did not speak the language, nor did he have hardly any contacts...

"I reconnected with a peer at The Economy of One series that I had not seen in ten years. We talked about what we were trying to do post-military. After the second session, he forwarded me a name of a contact that I recognized. The contact was a person I had worked with thirteen years ago and was now in the region (Bulgaria) working as a contractor. I reached out via LinkedIn to reconnect.

I reminded him of when we worked together, asked him if he remembered me, and let him know that I was thinking about retiring to the region and looking to meet and connect with quality people. I did not ask for a job, or even inquire to see if there were openings with his company.

A few weeks later, he responded. He remembered me and knew my reputation. The previous relationship, and previous job performance led him to offer me an interesting role. The role was not exactly what I was looking for, but strongly fit my skillset and experience. Based on my Economy of One training I recognized this opportunity as a mix between a potential opportunity and stopgap job. There was a possibility that the job would be something I was passionate about, I had the skills, I was marketable, and yet I did not have direct experience in the role.

I worked to craft a response to the initial inquiry that parsed my understanding of the requirements with experience I had that demonstrated proficiency in those areas. The goal was to supplement the mandatory resume with a document that better explained how my experience answered the requirements of the job. I got the job and started last week. If I had not bought into the network targeting method, I would have never made this contact, or thought about (considered) this opportunity."

You Need To Be Your Own Economy

The facts are that the economy has changed radically and so has the way businesses hire. There are now millions of people in transition who represent not only America's, but the world's largest—and growing—uninvested asset. We need a better solution. To provide one, we need to point out something obvious: that there is only one difference between someone who is unemployed and an entrepreneur. What is the difference? One has decided they have something to sell that is of value. So, each of us stands to gain by adapting the entrepreneurial mindset that we need to harness our unique value and drive demand in our own tiny economy of one. Consider these facts:

- 40% of today's workers will never go back to a corporate environment
- 40 million people in today's economy are self-employed (31% of the total workforce)
- 60 million are projected to be contract employees or "free agents" (one out of every two working will be contract employees)
- Up to 47% of ALL jobs will be automated in the next decade or so

These facts suggest that a new approach is required to create predictability in your opportunity pipeline. Our goal is to provide you the tools and processes that will show you exactly how to thrive in this new reality. We must adapt. Because the "system" as we know it is broken, technologies are accelerating change almost beyond comprehension, and global economic headwinds in most industries or developed countries are significant.

How Do People Make Money?

Today as you think about your future, the words flexibility, predictability and options are what matter most. It is important when you think about your future that you embrace an approach that provides as many options as possible. When people tend to think options, they tend to identify two, either get a job or start a business. *There are in fact six total combinations available to you that stem from one or a combination of these paths*! Please pause for a moment and rank in order your preferences from the following list. For example, you may be looking for a full-time job while willing to work as a "free agent" contract employee. You may decide to take a full-time job while starting a business on the side, you may take on contract "free agent" work to gain experience in an industry you are curious about while starting a small business based on using skills that you enjoy. These are just examples for you to consider. So, core options include:

- Free Agent
- Full-Time Employee
- Entrepreneur

What is best for you? For your family? Have you stopped to consider how different options might fit together to better compliment your long-term or short-term goals? Please take a moment and really think about it.

So, how are people now making money? In this new economy, people are:
- Holding out for the Holy Grail job with many benefits, but often coming up short
- Bundling together in social groups to help each other (small groups designed to encourage economic and socio-economic synergy between participants)
- Building portfolio careers: (Perhaps selling LegalShield®, while also being a realtor, while taking contract work as an event planner, all while writing your manuscript or movie idea)
- Diversifying income streams so that there's no over-reliance on any one source of income
- Accepting contract work in hopes it may develop into a full-time job

As you think about making money and moving forward, what do you see are the greatest personal or professional obstacles you may face? What options might be available to offset risks? How does your family life or commitments limit options or open relational doors to industries you want to explore? Things to consider:

-**Where are you in your professional life?** Are you starting a career, nurturing a career, at the end of a career, looking to get into a completely different industry, or use a completely different set of skills?

_____

_____

_____

_____

_____

_____

-**What defines your personal limitations?** Geography, finances, the need to support aging parents, children, physical (sickness) or health concerns, all may play an important role in your efforts to explore and define options.

_____

_____

_____

_____

-**What is your "definition of success"?** For some, it is all about money, ambition or promotion. For others it is about stability, the flexibility to work when you want, ability to travel anytime, security or the freedom of working for yourself. If it is early in your career, you may want your first "real job." When one of our participants answered the questions just listed, he realized that while he had been a highly paid executive, moving forward he didn't have the same definition of success that he had earlier in his career. In fact, he desired a job that gave him flexibility to spend more time with his grandkids and not travel so much. His definition of success had changed, as it was no longer driven by money or prestige. But he needed time to reflect on what this meant to his search.

_____

_____

_____

_____

_____

Confirm and explore your assumptions. We encourage you to visit with at least three people who know you well. Ask them about factors that you should consider in looking for opportunities and options to move forward. This counsel should serve as a solid sounding board in your decision-making process. Additionally, you may want to do an exercise we often advise people to engage in if they are struggling with identifying issues associated with this process.

Exercise 1: Where Have You Been and What Were Your Motives for Change?

If you are struggling to understand the career path or decisions you have made to this point, we suggest taking a piece of graph paper and making a simple timeline of the most recent companies you've worked for, with job titles. Under each company you worked for and job held, make a plus and minus column. Write everything you can recall about what you liked about the job, what skills you used that were "positive," perhaps awards you achieved, and also list items or issues that were negative.

If you are at the start of your career and can't reference actual roles, identify instead responsibilities or positions you've held that you have enjoyed (student council member, non-profit project volunteer, babysitter or summer painting crew, lifeguard, boy scout patrol leader.) Whatever experience you are referencing, it is fine. This is about "life experience" in roles, or assumed responsibilities that you engaged with, no matter where you are in age or in advancement within your career.

When you make this list you might find that you may have used skills that you enjoy at one particular job, or in one role, but maybe you didn't feel a fit with the culture of the company (or people that you worked with). As you consider one company and job title to the next, identify the motive that caused you to take the next job or opportunity. *What was your motive in taking each new role or job?* Was it a promotion, an opportunity to increase more desired skillsets, a necessary move? As you go through this exercise, again share your conclusions with someone who knew you at the time, or knows you well so that you can double check your assumptions with someone you trust who will "call you out" if indeed they remember differently. This exercise is valuable as it will cause you to remember what you have enjoyed, what you have not, and *why*. Once completed, file the sheet for future reference.

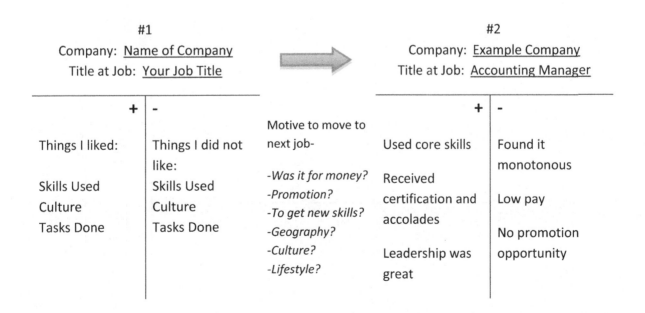

#1

Company: _____

Title at Job: _____

Motive to move to next job:

#2

Company: _____

Title at Job: _____

Motive to move to next job:

#3

Company: _____

Title at Job: _____

Exercise 1 Worksheet: Use additional paper if needed

Time Wasters

Here are ways to waste time when you are in transition:

- Job search websites
- Going to generic job fairs
- Job boards
- Sending generic resumes out to everyone you know
- Asking friends and family for their "help" when they don't even understand "the story of you" (which we define as exactly how you add value to companies by utilizing your best talent and to accomplish the job they need done, the way that they want it done, profitably)
- Classified ads (...or any other automated approach)

If you are one of many people who feel like they are sending their resumes into a Black Hole, guess what? You are! Your odds of getting the job when you apply online are 7 in 1,000... or less than 1%.

How the Resume Black Hole Works

Employers only post ads when they do not know who to hire through an *existing relationship*. Four out of five times, employers already know who they want and are simply fulfilling a regulatory stipulation by posting the opening. When they do post, hundreds of resumes overwhelm them. After people send in their resumes online, an algorithm or gatekeeper weeds down the pile as quickly as possible. Or, if HR lacks urgency to fill the job, they ignore the pile and wait to meet a candidate through a referral from someone they know.

Nobody Likes the Black Hole

Employers hate sorting the pile... and you hate being in it.

The Black Hole is Dangerous!

- It wastes your time
- It gives you a false sense of progress ("I have sent 57 resumes this week! I'm working so hard!")
- It reinforces your most paralyzing fears ("I have applied everywhere. Nobody will hire me!")

FACT: Relationships Get You Hired

What are the odds of landing the job if you have a referral? One in seven! In fact, 80% of new hires had one. Without any question, people do business with people they like and trust. This is the first rule of business. Talent often is not the primary reason why new hires "were awarded the opportunity." Did you catch that? The most talented people don't often get the job, it's those that are liked and trusted. You need an introduction, but how to get one?

You Have Been Focusing On "Networking," Right?

The rosy view of networking for opportunities: "a chance magical encounter that produces endless income," kind of like a magical watering can. If you are one of the people in the "holding out" group, you probably imagine that cultivating big relational networks to find income opportunities looks a bit like this. Maybe it's been your past experience: you larked upon a connection that referred you to a full-time permanent position. You felt lucky because it happened by random, *kind of like magic.*

In Reality It's About Relationships, Not Networks

Networking to build a large base of contacts (people in your network that you do not really know at all) is completely different than building a base of sincere and authentic relationships. Too often, most attend "big networking events" to feel productive, swapping cards with others who have no intention of following up. Building real relationships is not magic, but it does require intentionality. You will be happy to know it is possible to build measurable trust with others. The focus is about systematically cultivating relationships and converting them into opportunities, not hunting for the one magical connection. This course is about teaching you how to do the process with intention, so that even if you feel unlucky or uncertain, you'll still have opportunities. It's not just about finding one opportunity. Rather it is about making sure you will *always* have options.

Again, Relationships Will Get You Hired

Employers and potential entrepreneurial partners approach the relationship building process with the thought, "I want someone I can trust." They are putting their livelihoods, their business, into the hands of their employees or strategic alliances. But how can you tell who's trustworthy from a stack of resumes? Meanwhile, you are thinking, "I want to be treated as a person!" Both of these drives can align by harnessing relational paths, bypassing the automated algorithms.

Exercise 2: Hiring Practices

Over your entire career or experience of skill development, how many times have you been hired:

- From a referral or other relational connection?

_____

_____

- "Cold" through a job posting with no referral or contact at the company?

_____

_____

Know this: You are 20x more likely to get the job when you apply with a referral. If you do not have a referral, your competitor will!

How To Best Move Forward?

The best way to move forward is to figure out what you want (how you define an ideal opportunity). Understand how to ask people for their help to build relationships (building value for them while positioning yourself as a resource by telling the story of you). While this may sound simple, few people really grasp the mechanics of exactly how to do this in a methodical way. This will be discussed in detail in Module Four. Once you begin to engage with the process, you will use your accountability group to move forward in a systematic way to make measurable progress.

With THE ECONOMY OF ONE, You'll Learn How To...

- Cultivate authentic relationships, uncover new opportunities, and position your value
- Ask the right questions to deal with every person's unspoken agenda
- Create opportunities like an entrepreneur... through relationships
- Fill your pipeline full of opportunities so that you are never again out of options or at the mercy of job boards, HR or recruiters

What is CODE?

This is how to make measurable progress. We will teach you how to apply this structure to your opportunity search process:

C = Communicate

O = Organize

D = Document

E = Evaluate

THE ECONOMY OF ONE will break down your search for opportunity into a series of doable steps:

- Module One: Introduction-Creating Opportunities vs. Chasing Jobs
- Module Two: The Story of You
- Module Three: Relationships vs. Networks
- Module Four: Creating Personal And Professional Opportunities
- Module Five: Getting Started With Your MAP
- Module Six: The YBR
- Module Seven: Leaving A Good Footprint
- Module Eight: Negotiate Compensation And Close
- Module Nine: On-boarding
- Module Ten: Welcome To A New Way Of Life!

How Does CODE Work as Part of The Economy of One?

- It clarifies what to do and when to do it
- It teaches you how to play the right role for each step: Prospector/Headhunter and Connector, Technical Expert, Recruiter/Agent/Closer
- And, it gives you support, tools and templates, accountability, and a clear path for success

The CODE is 4 – 3 – 2 – 1

- Four phases: generate opportunities, position and qualify opportunities, propose and follow up, ongoing nurture of relationships
- Three roles: 1. Headhunter and Prospector 2. Connector and Technical Expert 3. Recruiter, Agent and Closer
- Two lists: the MAP and YBR
- One goal: to keep your pipeline of opportunity filled and moving!

Combining this system with an Accountability Partnership creates a dynamic mix of tools for success!

Exercise 3: CODE In Your Life

In your small group or on your own, ask yourself or discuss with another:

- How do I naturally tend to communicate?

_____

_____

- How do I organize my time?

_____

_____

- Based on what I now understand, what is my biggest obstacle to success? How comfortable am I with the process of creating documentation and holding myself accountable to goals?

_____

_____

_____

- From what I know now, what will CODE look like in my life? How does it change what I am doing or mindsets I've held to be true?

_____

_____

- What might be an obstacle to my success?

_____

_____

Internal Obstacles

Be honest: Did you have the courage to admit an internal obstacle to success? Interviewers can *sense* how you feel. We bring this up to simply help you realize that there are most likely issues you are going to need to work through. The good news is that you now have a safe place in which to do it. As you think about this, what do you sense, right now?

Change Happens Proportionate to Effort

Getting new results isn't just about changing what you're doing. It's about engaging new attitudes, skillsets and behaviors. We are going to help you assess where you are, identify what is most important to move forward step-by-step, and it will be accomplished in a safe environment.

Assignments for Next Session

- ☐ Review and complete Exercises 1-3 in Module One
- ☐ Review terms that you are unsure of in our terminology guide
- ☐ Review FAQ's associated with Module One to see if there's additional questions that you would like answered
- ☐ Make a list of potential accountability partners and bring it to class next week, or follow up with your assigned group

You are not alone. You are the solution. **You are an Economy of One!**

Module Two:
The Story Of You

Objectives for Today

By the end of this module, you will:

- Understand functionally what you want to do by removing title and sector (identifying "your passion")
- Review your "warehouse of skills," identifying your "best talent" (we define as what you are best at which is also hopefully the thing that you are passionate about and good at)
- Realize that a paycheck or earning money is a by-product of everything else being right. If you are able to position and articulate how your best talent (what you love to do and do best) will address exactly how you will make the business owner more money or deliver more value, then it becomes a mutual win
- Recognize transitional considerations like intrapreneurship, the concept of acting like an entrepreneur while working inside a traditional corporation. Do you really need to leave a company to create value? What are best choice options that honor where you are in life, what you value and what lowers your risks?
- Understand the role that corporate culture has in the hiring process, being able to describe where your personal style best fits in terms of type of corporate culture that is a "best fit" for you
- Be able to describe succinctly the "story of you" to others so that they will know how to function as your "banner wavers" in the marketplace
- Ask banner wavers for meaningful introductions to other quality people within their relationship base, positioning your value associated with the "story of you"
- Recognize any attitudes or behaviors that might cause you disconnect in asking for help from others
- Understand that this is the fourth most important decision you make in your life behind who or when to marry, whether to have kids or what role religion or faith plays in your life
- Describe in thoughtful detail what your ideal opportunity looks like
- Know how to "volunteer with a purpose"

So, You Think You Know The Story Of You? You Don't.

Let's be candid. If you asked your brother or sister (mother, father or best friend) to describe what it is you do, could they do it well? Could they say clearly exactly how you add value to an organization? More often than not, friends and family only understand at a very abstract high level where you have worked and the type of skills you have. Most people rely on their resume to "tell their story," which is the beginning of a terrible mistake when you are in transition.

- **The traditional resume is not the story of you: why?** Too often a generic resume is a list of skills and talent. It is a bunch of information that does not convey a story. It is a meaningless document because it has not been tailored to the needs of the person who is looking at it. It is a lot like a puzzle in that you have a bunch of pieces, but there is no "big picture" as it lacks clear direction or meaning.

- **What is the story of you?** It is the story you tell people about yourself that says clearly where you are passionate, the culture you are drawn to, and the talent and direct value you deliver business owners and leaders. It is dynamic and may change or be customized for the person (or the opportunity) to whom you are speaking.

- **Passion:** Think about the time in your life you were happiest personally and most productive professionally. Take time to really stop and remember how doing what made you happy made you feel. The feeling of contentment you are experiencing while reflecting on this memory are completely opposite to those that might make a "desperate jobseeker" feel powerless. In identifying the happiest time in your life professionally, often your "story" will map back to that time. This person and mindset associated with your most memorable time of success and happiness is who you want to align with in terms of mindset moving forward. This is the mindset you need to focus on in advance of an interview with a client or potential employer. Your desire is to go back to the place of being happy, confident and content with how you represent yourself professionally. The more you focus on how you feel when you feel empowered, you will begin to be aware of a shift and sense stronger professional alignment. This memory of where you were happiest in your career will help you to identify the type of culture you are attracted to as one that nurtures your person while engaging your passion. Focus on identifying a role you are performing, a role that you love (completely forgetting title). An organization is really a series of duties, functions and responsibilities. So, eliminating function, title and industry, think about duties and responsibilities. What role are you passionate about and how does this relate to what you want to do? Hopefully, it maps to your talent and what you excel at.

- **Why have the story of you clear?** Clarity for yourself and your own personal understanding is critical. Other people cannot help you if the story is not clear, so the most important "first relationship" you need to focus on is the relationship you have with yourself. As mentioned earlier, when even your family has no idea what you really do, you've got a problem if you are being honest, because often they are the first people to whom you turn for help! Also, you need a standard to measure the value of each opportunity against what you are passionate about, being extremely clear on what you really want (your perfect opportunity description). If you are unclear or uncertain, others that *you need to help* identify opportunity are set up for failure in assisting because they do not really understand your story. Once you work through the worksheet on refining your story, then you are able to share it with a few people to make sure it truly resonates and makes sense.

Who Are Your Banner Wavers?

Empower others to tell your story and activate your banner wavers! Once you get the story of you clear, you can empower others to tell it, asking them to help you expand, create and nurture a new base of relationships amongst people that they know. These other people who tell your story are what we call "banner wavers," those who assist you in identifying new opportunities that you otherwise would not have known about. You need banner wavers working on your behalf, telling your story to their relationships so that your opportunities for meaningful connections multiply.

Your goal is to convert your network and contacts into a relationship base. Understand we all have numbers of people we know. People earn their way into your relationship base (role of building trust and respect). Keep in mind that not everyone will convert from your larger network into a relationship base. In fact, only a select number of people will make the transition.

Intentionally Expanding Your Relationship Base

Does asking others for their help feel or seem odd? That's okay. Most people do struggle to ask for help from others, as it can seem uncomfortable if you approach it from a "what am I getting" standpoint. *We want you to focus on what you will be giving, which is the authentic ability to connect to others and add value to their world*. If someone asks you for help, do you typically turn them down? No? Well, stop and really think about it. *The average person will help you if asked*.

Also, how you ask makes all the difference. If you say to your banner wavers "I'm building my network and would like to meet other quality, like-minded people. Now that you know my story, can you think of people in your network that might be a good match for me to connect up with to simply visit with over coffee?" Keep in mind, you are not asking for a job (or acting like a "desperate jobseeker"). You are not asking the person you are meeting with for anything. You are simply telling your story, sharing yourself with them and seeing if there is anything you can do to help them expand or build their network. Since you are focusing exclusively on this, you are able to meet their next hire, resource, client or strategic partner. Reasons for the introduction? There can be many, such as you share industry experience, you are changing industries and want to better understand their role as you are making a transition, you'd like to learn more about their industry (do not characterize the meeting as an informational interview), you simply share things/ ideas/ values in common and would like to learn more about them professionally and personally. These reasons are solid reasons to make introductions for others, and if asked properly, your banner wavers or those in your accountability group should be happy to help expand your network of relationships.

The Story of You™ Examples

Before you begin, here are four sample responses to the assignment to write "the story of you."

These go from the worst example (A) to the best example (D). In reviewing these, they should provide to you an idea of the level of detail, and the approach required for the story of you to be meaningful to others. Do not be hesitant or question yourself. Just give yourself permission to write a simple working draft.

Example A: This gentleman runs a billion-dollar company. This is vague, incomplete and virtually useless.

An example of what **not** to do:

Passion:
Running a company

Best at:
Creating more profit

Culture:
Open

Example B: This person is a global IT professional. It is an "ok" example:

What are my passions?

- Growing businesses through addressing business development challenges and building/executing on sales transformation strategies
- Growing/mentoring sales leaders... (First line sales leaders have a critically important role in developing, inspiring, and retaining sellers)
- Working in an international, multi-cultural environment

What am I looking for in a corporate culture?

- A foundation in and a commitment to strong business ethics
- An organization who prioritizes clients, employees, and shareholders in that order
- A teaming and collaborative working environment

What am I best at?

I have tried to pick a few things that I like but have been reinforced by bosses, peers and employees...

- I take employee and customer contact to a relationship level through my engagement style and trustworthiness
- I translate technically complex offerings and products into client business value
- I have good personal and cultural sensitivity and inspire and lead teams
- I actively mentor and coach managers to improve their effectiveness

Example C: This person is an outside sales executive. It is a better example of the story of you:

Passion: I have been a geek / nerd for three decades. I love technology and love to be on the cutting edge of it. I was the first guy in the neighborhood with a computer, programming in UNIX in '91, was building websites on a dial-up modem, loved databases before they were cool, and currently my hobby is 3D printing. By the way, if you have not read much on 3D printing, this is our future in so many areas.

In short, I am a techie guy. With that said, I also like working with companies to make them more successful. This could be making them more profitable, reducing costs, streamlining processes. To do this takes a lot of questioning, research, problem solving and the ability to analyze the information and come up with a conclusion. Over the years I have used technology to work with my clients / companies.

Perfect Position: There are a few positions that I think fit my personality and skillsets. Technology sales would be the first, which is the position I am currently in. The next position would naturally be a VP of Sales with a technology company. Both positions can be found in Cerner, DST, or other similar companies. The last position would be a VP of Technology, working with a team of people inside an organization. This position could be found in a company where their focus may be to put out a product/service and my role would be to support the company. Hallmark would be a good example.

Culture: I've worked in small companies (less than 55 people) and medium size companies (over 300 people) and a large company (over 1000 employees). I have excelled in all. I think the key to the companies is the ability to address people, regardless of their job title or their position, and talk with them. Find out information about a process, project, etc... Even with the larger company, people knew who I was, had respect, and willing to work with you and provide information. That does not mean I would not fit into a Ford. I have never worked for this size of a company therefore I am not sure. I think it boils down to the fact I like to work. I like to spend my time with team members. I like to make the company, clients and departments successful. Because of that I have achieved respect and have had good to great working environments.

Example D: This person is a senior executive in manufacturing. This is the best example of the story of you:

My Passion
- Honest and Ethical Behavior.
- Operational Excellence.
  - Measuring and continuously improving every aspect of the business.
  - Reducing all losses within the organization.
  - Giving employees the support to achieve things that were thought to be impossible.
- Safety, Productivity, and Quality.
- Developing and introducing new technology with higher profit margins.

The Company Culture that I like:
- Organizations that have a clear vision and values.
- Organizations where issues are openly discussed, and plans made to address the issues.
- Organizations that lead their industry... even if they are not the industry leader.
- Organizations that want to improve and grow.

I am Best at:
- Employees
  - Improving Safety and Safety Awareness.
  - Improving Employee Engagement.
  - Managing and Developing Personnel.
  - Providing Guidance.
- Operations
  - Sales and Operational Planning.
  - Establishing Policies and Setting Goals.
  - Developing and Monitoring KPI's.
  - Data Trend Analysis and Reporting.
  - Strategic Planning: Growth and Cost Reduction.
- Financial
  - Budgeting and Forecasting.
  - Operating Cost Control.
  - Working Capital Management.
  - Developing and Prioritizing Capital Plans.

Exercise 1: Write The Story of You

Review the examples of The Story of You. As you can tell, some are very thoughtfully written. Other examples are not well done, and if anything come across as "generic" at best. Our goal in sharing these with you is to help you craft your story in a thoughtful way.

In preparation, think about the happiest time in your career professionally. What skills were you using? In what type of atmosphere were you working? Why did the culture of the company or assignment "feel right" to you? Beyond your title at the time, or the industry that you served, why did doing this role or using these skills bring you happiness or a sense of satisfaction?
Without over-thinking the details, list the top three skills you are passionate about, good at and contribute to companies you've worked for...

Top Three Skills:

1. A skill I am extremely passionate about:

_____

_____

_____

2. A skill I am <u>good</u> at:

_____

_____

_____

3. A skill I have that <u>adds to companies measurably</u> (adds profit, provided product innovation, expanded market share, leveraged existing strategic partners, created new strategic partners, diversified vendors, attracted new customers, provided new revenue streams, provided competitive advantage, helped attract employees or other talent, achieved process improvement, made my boss or team pleased, solved a problem, provided a much needed solution or fresh approach):

_____

_____

_____

Where Have I Been Happiest?

Identify three words that describe the culture or atmosphere of the working environment that makes you feel happy, secure, fulfilled, productive or content.

Working environments that make me feel happy and productive are:

1. _____

2. _____

3. _____

Now reference your answers as you write The Story of You.

- What can you tell your audience about job choices you have made or skills that you have, to help them better understand how you have made choices that illustrate your passion?

_____

_____

_____

- If you are looking for a new industry, why? Address how your background or experiences connect or prepare you for where you would like to go?

_____

_____

_____

- Maybe you have never worked in an environment you've truly enjoyed culturally. So, when you think of companies that have cultures you admire, what specifically is it about their culture that you are drawn to? Why is it a "good match"?

_____

_____

_____

_____

On the next page, write your version of "The Story of You."

The Story of _____

_____

_____

_____

_____

_____

_____

_____

_____

_____

_____

_____

_____

_____

_____

Exercise 2: Share Your Story With Someone You Trust

Before moving to Module Three, tell a few people you trust your newly refined "Story of You." Ask them if there is anything that surprises them in hearing the details of your story. Ask them if they feel they could repeat it to other people accurately. Then ask them to be thinking about people in their networks of good friends and relationships that might want to meet you. Why would their friends and relationships want to meet you? They would want to meet you because you are proactively expanding your base of quality relationships. In this process you will most likely meet people who could be their next client or employer. Does this make you feel nervous? It is okay. You will simply tell them that you are looking to meet other quality people. So, why would they want to meet you? You are expanding your relational network and may be meeting their next client, employer or friend that could be helpful to them. In a world that focuses on quantity, you need to convey that you are focused on quality relationships. This makes you valuable amongst those that they consider their "network."

Exercise 3: Re-Visit Your Path(s)

Which path (or combination) of paths was your top choice from Module One (see list below)? Your second choice? Now that you have had time to really think about it, has anything changed? Connect your top two choices with brackets:

- ☐ Free Agent
- ☐ Full-Time Employee
- ☐ Entrepreneur

Exercise 4: Your Warehouse of Skills

Inventory your personal capital and "best talent." Think over your life. List 3-5:

Past positions and industries (if you did the graphic timeline exercise in Module One, please refer to this prior exercise):

_____

_____

_____

Roles, responsibilities and skillsets you used or developed for each key role or position (+ or -):

_____

_____

_____

Ways you have been challenged (+ or -):

_____

_____

Areas or experiences in which you really excelled, received acknowledgement or enjoyed:

_____

_____

Exercise 5: Identify Your Passions

A passion is anything you love to do. What are yours? Make a list. For now, do not worry if you can find a job or new business associated with it.

What got you really excited as a kid? What about now?

_____

_____

_____

If money were not an issue, what would you do every day? How do current industries or career paths, or options align with this passion?

_____

_____

_____

What makes you want to face today? What motivates you? How do you define success?

_____

_____

_____

Also, list what de-motivates you:
Roles and responsibilities that challenge in more negative than positive ways:

_____

_____

Topics you find boring:

_____

_____

Environments you find stressful:

_____

_____

_____

What puts you on autopilot or makes you anxious?

_____

_____

Exercise 6: Your Marketability

List 5+ skills you have used to make business owners money or yourself money. Include previous jobs or projects, volunteer or part-time work, classes taken, your hobbies, etc.

_____

_____

_____

_____

_____

_____

Which skills and talents:
- Have you been paid for?

_____

_____

_____

_____

_____

- Could you be paid for?

_____

_____

_____

_____

- Are second nature to you?

_____

_____

_____

_____

What do you consider your "best talent"? We define "best talent" as the one primary skillset you have that adds measurable value and profit to those that might employ you (either full time, as a contract to hire employee or as an entrepreneur). Identify three specific circumstances you can think of where you have used this best talent to add measurable value and profit to those you have worked with.

_____

_____

_____

_____

Do you have a skill may look unmarketable? Be open-minded! Some people *blog* for a living!

_____

_____

_____

_____

Exercise 7: Your Opportunity Spreadsheet

Grab all the items from Exercises 1-6, write them down here and later put them in a spreadsheet. For each one, check off: passionate, skilled, and marketable. This is your *personal capital*.

Personal Capital Item	Passionate	Skilled	Marketable	Application

Personal Capital Item	Passionate	Skilled	Marketable	Application

Now, fill in the "Application" column according to these formulas:

- Passionate + Skilled = Volunteer
- Skilled + Marketable = Stopgap Job
- Passionate + Marketable = Future Job
- All three = Your Perfect Type of Opportunity!

Your opportunity target lies at the intersection of your passion, skills, and marketability. It is your sweet spot.

Exercise 8: Describe Your Perfect Opportunity

Your perfect opportunity is what you would love to do and get paid for. Combine the results from Exercise 1 (on page 30) and Exercise 5 (on page 34), considering the path you want plus the intersection of the perfect opportunity you identified in your spreadsheet. What does this opportunity look like?

_____

_____

_____

_____

_____

Employees, freelancers, and business owners think about work differently. Generally, they either have a "Job," (paycheck or Opportunity) a "Project," or a "Lifestyle" mindset. Which do you want to look for?

_____

_____

Write your perfect opportunity description. Include optimal pay or earning potential, the skills / best talent you would use, and the solutions you'd provide along with the type of business, industry or client you would like to serve. Try to be as specific as possible in your descriptions.

_____

_____

_____

_____

_____

_____

_____

_____

Compare the new opportunities you find as you follow the process to this description to check what they have in common. This description of the "perfect opportunity" becomes a measure in which you apply to each opportunity to determine the level of personal fit. Did this exercise surprise you? Did it confirm a direction that you have thought about for some time? Did it reveal a direction you wouldn't have really considered?

_____

_____

_____

_____

_____

_____

The 70/30 Rule: Work and Volunteer

While in transition, we suggest that you volunteer your professional skills with approximately 30% of your time. You will advance your career while helping others.

Why volunteer? It will help you be productive and feel better about yourself. It will extend your relational network during your job search. It will also help you bulk up your portfolio of skills and deliverable solutions. You will be able to see if a new industry is really a fit for you by having the chance to explore freelancing before investing capital. When you give, you become more valuable in the eyes of others. Givers create opportunities and develop new relational connections with others.

Optional Homework Assignment

Mock interview someone who knows you well. Ask them about you:

- How would you describe me?
- When have I seemed happiest in life? What was I doing at that time?
- When I have seemed happy giving to others, what was I doing? What skills was I using? Where should I consider voluntary work while I am in transition? How could this volunteer work help me moving forward?

Assignments For This Module

☐ Review Module Two Handout: Examples of The Story Of You

☐ Write your Story of You: Understand this is a work in progress. Too often people "over think" this exercise and fail to engage because they get lost in the process. Do not do this. Just start jotting things down and stay focused on roles or duties that brought you joy, regardless of title or industry. Do not "write The Story of Your Life," keep your descriptions of what you like to do very concise and be thinking about how each of the things you like to do aligns with skills you enjoy using

☐ Share your story with a close friend to assess their reaction, tweak appropriately

☐ Now, practice your story with several people to see if they understand and can feel confident in explaining your story to others

☐ Who could be your "banner wavers"? List your top 10 people to contact (think about your good friends, people who you've volunteered with, people that you've worked closely with, who are in your neighborhood or PTA, people you went to school with, worked with in past jobs, friends from childhood). Identify your top 10 banner wavers (if you cannot think of 10, start with a target of five and plan to expand it to 10)

☐ Review any terms you might not understand

☐ Complete the eight Exercises, putting sincere time and thought into your answers as these exercises are very revealing

☐ Write your "perfect job description" on an index card or piece of paper and put it at eye level where you work at home so that you see it regularly, share this with your accountability group

Module Three: Relationships vs. Networks

Objectives

By the end of this module, you will know:

- How to discern the difference between a trusted relationship and a vaguely defined "network"
- How to create, expand and nurture relationships (each is a different behavior and skillset)
- How to be your own Headhunter, Connector and Prospector
- How to address your attitudes of uncertainty or lack of confidence in approaching others for help
- Facts about relationships as they relate to creating personal and professional opportunities
- The difference between "building a network" and focused effort at nurturing relationships
- How to teach people to position you as a resource, not a "desperate jobseeker"
- How to activate your "banner wavers" to expand your network of quality relationships
- How to recognize healthy relationships versus unhealthy relationships or behaviors

Relationships Are Everything

If you have been in transition for any amount of time, you have most likely heard ad nauseam about the importance of building your "network." Typically to build a "network," people focus on quantity of people within the network rather than the quality of people that they truly know. The result is that people have large networks of essential strangers that they met at a "networking event." They swapped cards and never engage in further follow-up.

While the size of your network is important, associating with a large group of people you really do not know instills a very dangerous and real false sense of security. Research suggests that the typical Facebook user has 433 "friends," three or four of which *might* show up in the *most dire of circumstances* to *actually help* you. Stunning isn't it? What needs to be stressed here is that there is a significant difference between a network of *vaguely associated people* and that of "trusted relationships." Since focus is often on the quantity of people in our networks, we don't readily recognize the steps required to truly "build" relationships. This issue of changing your relational aim to focus on creating and nurturing a smaller pool of people who share mutual trust, values and respect is a *critical* take away from this course. We intend to forever change the way you look at and define the words "relationship" and "networking," as our goal is to help you build meaningful relationships, grounded in trust, within a healthy and expanding network. (We do not want you to build a large network, occasionally finding someone that you can have a relationship with when you are in "dire circumstances." Too often this is when you suddenly conclude that you "need" people or their help).

Definition of networking:

1. People you have met, a collection of names and business cards (you can accomplish the same thing by picking up the White Pages)

2. Is a brainless activity for salespeople looking for a coffee date

3. It is an organized form of "card swapping," where participants usually have no intention of additional follow up

Definition of relationships: Comprised of individuals that possess mutual trust, values and respect. They share a genuine interest in the success of one another *personally and professionally*.

What is the difference between "banner wavers" and general relationships in your network?
Your banner wavers *know how to position you professionally to actively introduce you to others.* Those in your network who you have a relationship with may not know how to professionally position you. While you do have a relationship with them, they are not a "banner waver" unless they are making introductions into their network on your behalf.

Stop and consider this new definition of "relationship." How many people do you know right now (at this moment) that *genuinely care* about you personally and professionally? How many would "show up for you" in the case of real need? This is an important question because when you are in transition, it is when you find out who are your true friends. Ponder this and then contrast this short list with the approximate size of your "network" on LinkedIn, Twitter or Facebook or Instagram. When you apply this new definition of relationship, often it suggests that a lot of *sincere work* remains to be done on the relationship to move people effectively from your "network" pool to that of true "relationships."

So how do you *feel* about the idea of creating and nurturing new relationships? For some people (especially introverts), the thought of committing energy and time to creating and nurturing relationships can seem almost overwhelming. Is this you? For people who are extroverts, it also can be challenge when we consider everything that our lives require of us. Both introverts and extroverts universally struggle at times because as hard as it can be hard to get out of your comfort zone to create a relationship, it can be equally difficult to prioritize the time and focus that nurturing a relationship requires. These obvious issues acknowledged, you should commit to the idea of expanding and nurturing relationships no matter where you are in the stage of the game. What this means is that even when you feel you are through a "transition," you need to stay fully *committed* to this process of building and nurturing relationships because the next round of personal and professional opportunities for you may be a result of the coffee you are having this morning!

People (*all people*) can truly help one another as the ability to help is truly independent of one's station in life. To illustrate its importance, consider for a moment the following story:

Frank and The Deck Builder

Early in Frank's recruiting career he found it difficult to distinguish himself from the many other people that served in his field. Frustrated with this, he was pondering his future when a deck builder he had hired showed up one hot summer afternoon to work on repairing his back deck. After a bit, Frank decided the guy might like something cold to drink. Frank stepped out on his deck with a glass of iced tea and discovered something that *forever changed* the way he looked at relationships.

Through casual conversation, Frank shared a few details about his work as a recruiter and the deck builder thoughtfully took note. He offered to introduce Frank to a few people he thought Frank might enjoy knowing. Frank agreed, unaware that these *casual introductions* from the guy who repaired his back deck would be associated with what would become the highest profile accounts in his block of business! *These are people that Frank never would have naturally approached unless it had been for the kindness of the deck repairman.* What did Frank learn? *Anyone, in any station of life, anywhere, can truly help you if you are focused on connecting as people, looking for ways to genuinely relate to one another personally and professionally.* Read this sentence again at least three times...

Position Yourself As You Meet Others

How do you position yourself as a resource instead of a "desperate jobseeker" when you are building your relationship base and asking your banner wavers for introductions into their networks? Begin by *not mentioning your job transition* (at all). This may sound so very counterintuitive, but it is a critical point that cannot be emphasized enough. When you meet new people, you want to focus on the story of you. You want to be able to speak to your value and provide resources to the person so that your motives are not being questioned. *Why do this?* Do it because it leaves people with a positive impression of who you are as a person instead of leaving them with a vaguely written resume that they never asked for.

What if they already know you are in transition? If the other person already knows that you are in transition, then do address the issue if it arises, but do it with tact. Say something to this effect "Yes, I am in transition. And while I am not looking for a J-O-B or "Just Another Paycheck," I am looking for an opportunity. I define an opportunity as something that really excites me as it adds strong profit and value to any company or person I might work with. So, yes, if I came across a real opportunity with the right company or individual, I certainly would entertain the idea or offer. However, right now I am focused on expanding my relational network for the purpose of meeting new people. Since I am building my network, many of these people may be your next client, friend or opportunity. Here's the type of people I'd like to meet...Do you know of anyone in your network of relationships that might be a good fit?"

Call Or Introduction Reluctance

At this point, natural worries include the nagging internal questions: *What have I got to offer? What if they don't want to meet me?* People worry endlessly that when they go to meet someone that they will have nothing to offer. This can be especially true if you are currently in transition or have been in transition for a long time. The premise though to any meeting or introduction must be this golden rule:

> **Whenever two quality people get together there is an exchange of mutual value. Money is anything you can do to solve a problem for someone else! So, in meeting them you are looking to make an investment. You want to identify what they need, providing value to them in a tangible way. The initial value is this: that you are two quality people! When two quality people get together, therein exists an exchange of value.**
>
> **Authenticity counts! What is *extremely* valuable is that you are willing to meet and you are willing to offer part of yourself to another with sincerity. To invest time in another human being is extremely powerful. Time is something you can never get back, so the act of investing time in another person is truly priceless in and of itself.**

This is not about quid quo pro or keeping score. It is about meeting all quality people regardless of their station in life. Whenever two quality people get together, there's value. Find out what is meaningful to people. But you mentally protest: I don't have anything to "give." It is not about keeping score. It is about mutual value. How can you know what you have to offer *until you ask* what is meaningful personally and professionally to the person? The fact: you do not know until you ask.

How To Convert Your "Network" Into A Base Of Relationships

So how do you discover what a person needs most? Here is a simple but profound idea: Ask what a person needs most and give it to them. How do you do this? By asking them open-ended questions and listening carefully to what the person is *really* saying. Questions such as:

- **Tell me about yourself**…What key elements do they focus on in telling you their story? What are their passions? What types of experiences and corporate cultures have they worked for? Desired companies? What do they get excited about? Come prepared to the meeting having already reviewed their LinkedIn profile or Facebook page to learn more about them.
- **What are the biggest challenges with your current role, position, company, or industry?** What are your personal or professional challenges? What types of resources, introductions or connections would be helpful in your current role(s)? Your boss?
- **Tell me about your wife, spouse, significant other, family and kids.** Is your child / peer/ sister… looking for a mentor? An internship? His/her next opportunity?   I am considering introductions to others in my relationship base who may help them get to their next stage of professional or personal growth.
- **What might cause them to move forward with personal or professional goals?** What is your definition of "success"? How might I help make success more readily happen for you? What types of relational connections might help the most? What type of opportunities are they looking for? What is the company they work for struggling with? What is their passion? Their story? Where culturally do they fit in and how do they add value to companies? What is their core talent and who in your relationship base needs to know about it?

Make a list of people while you are talking (target 3-5 names) who you feel they would benefit by meeting once you discover more about the person and what they need.

Become a Connector and Headhunter or "Prospector" for Others

When you are thinking about others and their needs, your goal in serving them is to identify how you can help them personally or professionally and then DO IT! It sounds simple but *execution* is everything.

How is this accomplished? The first key thing is that you need to be responsive and available to others. While it sounds obvious, you would be stunned with the number of people who fail on these two fronts. Why? Because we have so many methods of electronic touch point (email, messenger on Facebook, texting, voice mail, tweeting, etc...) it is easy to lose focus on the best method or preferable method by which to communicate with people.

What do we mean when we suggest "be available" to people? What we mean is to *take the call* when people are trying to reach you! Do not send them to voice mail when talking is inconvenient (yes, Millennial, we are talking to you!). When we say be responsive, what we mean by this is to get back to people within 24 hours of their effort to communicate with you. Why do this? *Because most people do not do it*! Seriously, most people are extremely sloppy in their communication, not following up or following through with commitments that should be priority. When you do extend this courtesy to others, the relationship foundation begins to form because people sense you are simply available, prompt and interested in their needs.

60/30/10 Rule

What types of people will you meet when you actively expand your relationship base?

Our experience suggests 60% of people you meet will "do what you do for them if you do it for them first," which we define as a "quid quo pro" type of relationship. This is not preferable as you want to seek people who recognize the value of the relationship itself and aren't "scorekeepers."

30% are total narcissists and your meeting will be all (and only) about them. Indicators that "it is all about them."

- Lack of eye contact
- Show up late, check their phone, text and or take calls while you are meeting (visibly distracted)
- Conversational focus that has a disproportionate amount of time on "them" and their story instead of you and your story (they aren't asking questions and don't seem to care to listen to your replies)
- The conversation has a selfish sub-context that you can feel, which feels like "poor chemistry," keep in mind that statistical research suggests two in every ten people will not "like" you no matter what you do, so if it's the case and you perceive it, don't be hard on yourself as this happens on occasion and is a function of the numbers of people you meet with

- You felt they were "pushing an agenda" and it simply turned you off

And finally, there's the "sweet 10%." These people are responsive, available, and open to establishing a professional and personal relationship with you based on mutual respect. What are indicators that you are working with someone who might fall in the sweet 10%?

- They share values, background or connections and affiliations with you
- You have "good personal chemistry" with them
- They seem selfless in their behavior
- There is two-way dialog and reciprocal appreciation of small gestures of kindness or sincerity
- You genuinely like them
- You recognize a synergy and clear ways in which a relationship with them would be mutually beneficial

In interacting over time, what are you looking for from the other person? You are looking to see how sincere the person is before they would be moved from your "network" to "relationship base" category. Time will afford you the opportunity to verify or see if they are true to their personality. You will see if they follow through, if they are available and responsive to you and most importantly, if what they say lines up with how they behave. *Often people claim to "be into building relationships" but once you have coffee with them, there's no further activity or effort.* You are looking for people who are not only good at the initial conversation, but also the second and third conversation where, if going well, the trust and rapport is measurably building over each interaction. If you find that they aren't really about relationships, and are hesitant to put in the time required, then don't waste your time further and move on. In the next module, we will tell you exactly the process you need to engage to identify and create specific opportunities within your relationship and banner waver base.

Time Plays A Critical Role In This Process

Creating and nurturing relationships is a lot like dating someone in that you can't learn everything about someone over a single coffee. It may take several interactions before you decide that this is a good fit, but it's well worth the investment of time to determine this. To accomplish nurturing a relationship, you need to focus on building trust. How do you accomplish this? There are several ways:

- Identify specific ways in which to help them or "give them what they need," and then do it!
- Ask personal questions at the beginning of every discussion so that it is obvious you care about them personally
- Be real around them and demonstrate vulnerability by admitting what you may "not know" or "need help with," things that they can provide. People always desire to help those humble enough to ask. Be one of those people who ask for help and risk vulnerability
- Be genuine. Let it be obvious that making everyone happy isn't your priority, that you are confident in who you uniquely are and are unashamed of it
- Speak and offer help or advice when you really have something to say, not just to fill space. People who are genuine measure their words, and are sincere in their communications

- When you mess up in the process of nurturing a relationship, say so. Own it and take responsibility for whatever has happened in such a way that you offer a sincere apology and recognition of the issue if there is a misunderstanding or area in which you've been negligent (grossly late for a meeting for example)
- Be transparent with people; don't harbor "secondary agendas" as you interact with them
- Speak plainly and clearly with them in methods they prefer (if they like Facebook and LinkedIn, connect with them in channels that remind them you care and are tracking with them, their families, interests, etc...)
- Don't hesitate to check in with people by voice mail. Leave brief messages that simply let people know you are thinking about them and are wondering if they need anything. Say that you don't expect them to return the call unless there's anything you can do for them, but that you wanted to check in with them and simply say hello
- Follow up on details associated with every conversation. If you need to email an article, email it. If you need to make an introduction for them, do so promptly. If you have a tool that will help them, send it. Don't identify a way and offer to help them then not follow through, as it will rapidly undo the trust you've worked hard to achieve
- Give first to others and give *frequently*. Don't keep score but always look for ways in which you can personally and professionally enrich the lives of others

Investments in others take time to compound and gain interest, but these investments are well worth making. To quote a book that captures a lot of truth, be a "Go-Giver" not a "Go-Getter" (*Go-Givers Sell More* by Bob Burg and John David Mann). This is an excellent read and reference if you tend to struggle with this idea.

Exercise 1: Relational Self-Assessment And Discussion

How do you feel about the process of creating, nurturing, or expanding relationships?

Where do you excel in building relationships?

Where do things tend to fall apart? Do you struggle to create, nurture or maintain relationships?

What do you feel will be most difficult for you in addressing areas where you can change attitudes or improve skills and behaviors?

Make a list of 3 specific obstacles to your success based on attitudes you have about the process, skills you need to improve, or behaviors you suspect need to change. How can your accountability group help you overcome obstacles to your success?

Obstacles to Success:

1.

2.

3.

Key Recommendations:

The biggest problem we see amongst those we coach is nurturing. Why? It is the area of biggest inconsistency that most people struggle with. The problem tends to stem from not understanding what nurturing is or how to do it properly. The primary reason people do not nurture relationships is the notion that a phone call to check in or to say hello is "bothering" the person or self-serving. The exact opposite is true!

While we encourage you to focus on professional side of nurturing, keep in mind it is only half of the formula. Here is an example of how the personal side of relationships really makes a difference in professional settings...

Tom's Story...

Tom was a quiet engineer and a new hire to a major corporation working with many new teams. One individual who also was a professional engineer was often assigned to be a member of Tom's working teams, but Tom invested little time getting to know really anything about the person on a personal level. As engineers are known to have differing opinions, increasingly things became tense between Tom and this colleague. Often their professional viewpoint on varying professional matters disagreed.

At a critical point of team decision-making, Tom's colleague proceeded to go around Tom on a key decision and managed to further isolate the relationship by positioning for power amongst other peers participating on the project. At the advice of Tom's wife (and after some soul searching), he reached out after hours to ask his colleague to join him for dinner. At dinner, Tom apologized for not having taken time to get to know his teammate and sincerely tried to patch things up. Did Tom have to do this? No. Was this his exclusive problem or were both men equally guilty of not fostering a personal relationship? Clearly both were responsible, but Tom decided to be the "bigger person" and mend the fences with his teammate. From this point forward the tension was diffused and both men were able to relate to one another beyond the professional sandbox. Tom and his colleague intentionally sought to identify common ground between them and not focus on the issues that separated them or their professional viewpoints. This willingness to address the tension, to apologize, and reverse the trajectory of the working "relationship" made the entire team more productive and through this, Tom learned a valuable lesson. Personal relationships matter! While they take initial and ongoing effort, they are a lot easier to properly manage at the beginning if you simply take time and make the investment. He did not make the mistake again.

Please Reflect on These Questions and Jot Down Your answers:

- What type of attitudes might surface when I meet new people that I could improve on?

- Ask: Am I quick to judge? Am I hesitant to invest in others until they prove themselves to me? Am I motivated only by what they can do for me?

_____

_____

- What are the common excuses I make for myself that my accountability partners need to "call me on" when they see these things happening in relationships? (For example: I say nurturing is important, but then I "get busy" and don't actually do it…) Take a moment to list them here:

_____

_____

_____

- Behaviors that need to change or improve for me to build trust with others:

_____

_____

_____

- Skills I need to work on:

_____

_____

_____

Exercise 2: Goals to Create and Nurture New Relationships

- Identify realistic goals for the next week and next month. Considering your time commitments, what % of your time will you commit to creating new relationships? To nurturing existing current relationships? What specifically does this look like in your schedule? Consider the goal of making 5 calls before 5:00pm.

_____

_____

_____

Exercise 3: Getting Started By Listing Your Top 25 Relationships

Take a few minutes to reflect on the names that you listed as your banner wavers and now add to this list. Off the top of your head, list 20 additional names of people within 10 minutes to whom you feel you should reach out.

You will refer to this list in Modules Five and Six: Getting Started: Applying What You've Learned. (MAP and YBR.)

1.	11.
2.	12.
3.	13.
4.	14.
5.	15.
6.	16.
7.	17.
8.	18.
9.	19.
10.	20.

Assignments for Next Session

☐ Discuss this section and answers to the questions for reflection with your accountability partners. Address what you feel are your biggest obstacles for success and brainstorm about how you can support each other in making necessary changes to address your goals

☐ Schedule time in your daily calendar to create and nurture new relationships

☐ Meet with your accountability partner(s)

☐ Begin asking your banner wavers for assistance in positioning your value with their relationships

☐ Place your list of banner wavers and top 25 relationships in a place that is easy to remember and accessible as you will refer to this list in Modules Five and Six

☐ Next up, Creating Personal and Professional Opportunities

Module Four: Creating Personal And Professional Opportunities

Objectives

By the end of this module you will know:

- How to use your ideal opportunity description to avoid "retrofitting" yourself to fit a job description (indicators that indeed you are doing this)
- How to use strategies designed to identify or uncover your ideal opportunity
- How to describe exactly the type of company you want to talk to, and you will identify the type of problem they have that you are uniquely qualified to solve with your "best talent"
- How to be your own Agent and Technical Expert
- The mindset, attitudes, and behaviors of an Agent
- How to position your best talent, going direct to companies and people that need it as either a contractor, potential employee, or entrepreneurial resource
- As a Technical Expert, how to communicate your value and "qualify" companies, opportunities or contract opportunities where both parties recognize mutual value, establishing in the process "right fit"
- How to *dramatically focus* your efforts so you do not chase "unqualified" jobs or opportunities
- How to hire someone to do research on companies for you if you are uncertain how to do this on your own
- How to reach out and establish relationships with people who are in a position or an industry that you are interested in or would like to pursue
- Strategies to overcome attitudes and behavior barriers that contribute to "call reluctance," or sense of fear in asking others for help
- How to set realistic weekly and monthly goals that will help you to make measurable progress
- How to best utilize your accountability group to strategize on how to go direct to companies or people in positions to whom you want to speak

Retrofitting Yourself to Fit a Job Or "Opportunity"

Are you tempted to retrofit who you really are to fit a job description, to what HR said, or to what the job board described? You may be thinking to yourself "If I'm not what they say they want then I won't hear from them." *This is not where your focus should be when trying to uncover opportunity.*

Where should your focus and intent be?

Start by recognizing that HR won't let you actually talk to the people who really understand the work that needs to be done, or often even who you would report to! These issues acknowledged; you still need to know what is really behind the job description. How? An excellent way to get around this natural barrier is to go direct to people currently at the company in the role you are interested in, and ex-employees who have been in the role. Current and previous employees are your best source of information. LinkedIn Premium will identify past employees of any company they have on record and reaching out through Linkedin in-mail is a strong option to engage in dialog with them.

What are other factors that contribute to you feeling a need to retrofit yourself? Often to make progress while facing transition, the temptation is to choose "quantity over quality" in terms of engaging methods to move forward. Here is a list of indicators of the "quantity over quality" behavior surfacing:

- You spend hours on the internet mindlessly surfing for the "right online job application or posting"
- You send in resumes (endlessly) and work hours on "customizing" cover letters for companies that never respond
- You attend every networking session in town, but are not focused on the most important aspect of building your relationships, which is to follow up past an initial meeting (a strong tendency for extroverts who feel comfortable meeting others, but may lack the discipline to put in the time to get to know the person further)
- You do the complete opposite of attending network sessions and instead stay home preferring to be "busy online" (hiding behind a screen) instead of investing time with people who might help you (strong tendency for introverts who don't feel comfortable meeting new people)
- You see jobs posted where you *might* be a fit, but the job really does not excite you. *You apply anyway*

Do these statements describe your attitudes or behaviors? Do you struggle to really define what you are really looking for? The notion that simply putting in enough time and effort, responding to everything to "find a job or opportunity," will produce good results, is an *extremely dangerous and destructive mindset*. Why? Because, too often you will find you invest a tremendous amount of time in the effort (quantity) with little focus (quality). This type of behavior contributes to the feeling of being *busy*, yet the outcome is often *completely unproductive*. How and why does this happen?

It begins when you inadvertently lose sight of what you really want. In reviewing numerous options, you become tempted to "retrofit" yourself to *any* company or job description that might work, and then you sense that you are increasingly becoming subservient to a system that inherently feels demeaning to you. You try to fit everything in terms of "job descriptions," and the net result is that you focus on nothing, which leads to an endless loop of completely unproductive activity. The longer the time you spend in this seemingly endless loop, often the more frustrated or discouraged you can become. We believe this is one key factor that contributes to many people (estimated 23 million in the U.S. alone) just quitting the job search process all together.

It's Time To Get Radical

Here are several key reasons why you need to be radically focusing, using your time and resources very strategically:

Contender vs. Pretender – When you identify and apply for something that truly excites you, you are a contender for the position not a pretender trying to persuade someone that you are really interested and the right candidate. The bottom line? People can *sense* your level of conviction. If you are retrofitting yourself into a job, or what even may seem like an "opportunity" but you aren't *genuinely* excited about it, people can sense it and it works against you in the interview process.

Human Burnout Is Real – In a time of transition, you are wired for *only so much* professional rejection. Repeated rejection can lead to a sense of being without purpose, which should be addressed immediately if you begin to sense this is surfacing in your emotions and state of mind. We have found that while burnout is real, you need safe outlets in which to interact and let go of and examine what's "not working." Accountability groups are so critical to this process. They provide a natural sounding board, a safe place to "say how you really feel about an experience that went south," and a place for people to gently remind you it is time to move forward, no matter how difficult, traumatic, or trying the experiences that you've had to this point.

If you feel a lack of urgency or sense of avoidance, always ask yourself: Where has every personal and professional opportunity you have ever had come from? If you think about it, the overriding answer is relationships! You need to stay radically focused on expanding and nurturing relationships as this is CRITICAL no matter where you are in the stage of the game. Every personal and professional opportunity you have coming may originate from the coffees you are having this morning. So, quit complaining about the time involved, and go sip a nice cup of coffee! What are the methods to create opportunity?

Ways to Identify Or Create "Opportunity"

Do you struggle to get your head around the idea of "creating opportunity"? Some people really do have a hard time believing that there is a process to truly uncover opportunity. But be assured that the process does exist, and there is a "step by step" way in which to follow it. Remember, it is suspected that up to 80% of jobs or opportunities aren't posted, so how do you uncover them? How do you position your best talent and drive demand amongst companies or individuals willing to compensate you for it? How do you think like an entrepreneur, positioning your unique value to uncover opportunity for work, employment, or income? There are several different strategies you can engage to move forward and make measurable progress, including:

- Thinking like an agent and going directly to companies that need your best talent
- Talking to people direct within companies doing what you want to do
- Talking to people in your individual relationship base with contacts in industries or positions you want to explore, and identifying people to talk to in their sub-relationship base

- Identifying people who are ex-employees of companies you are interested in that held the role, and talking to them about how to position yourself and who you should reach out to at the company
- Call experts or those calling direct on companies with knowledge, who can then refer you to people and sources within industries and companies of interest
- Act with the confidence of an entrepreneur (identify a problem you are uniquely qualified to solve), and position your best talent to create measurable company value (such as new revenue, market advantage, strategic leverage, etc…), going direct to people and companies as a Prospector, Technical Expert, and Closer to drive demand for what you can uniquely supply

We will discuss each of these strategies in detail. Helpful tools such as scripts or email templates have been provided as downloads associated with this module so that you can use them to accelerate your efforts.

Method 1: Get Your Banner Wavers To Introduce Their Relationships

There is a *significant difference* between positioning you as a true resource, and that of a desperate jobseeker. When you work with your banner wavers to understand the story of you and your best talent, it is critical that they think about these things in relation to the type of people that would really benefit from knowing about you (not just offer you a job). Your goal in helping them to understand the story of you, and your best talent, is to help them effectively position you within trusted relationships in their network and sub-networks of relationships.

How do you teach your banner wavers? By explaining the "story of you" and asking them to *repeat it back to you* so that you are *confident* that they can position you properly with *anyone* they introduce you to. If you are looking for introductions into a specific industry of interest, or to specific types of people who are in certain roles, *don't fail to ask who your banner wavers know that fit this description* as this might jump start their thinking against a short list of introductions that they can make on your behalf. What if they know of a job for which they think you will be a good fit? Well, that's fine, but make sure that they say what you are looking for is <u>an opportunity</u>, not a job.

You are looking to add measurable value to a company that can appreciate and reward you for your contributions and capabilities. This immediately moves you out of the realm of common HR conversations into more strategic dialogs with management about the implications of your vision and the specific value you could deliver to the company (which is a completely different conversation than talking about a position they happen to have available.) What if the position that your friend knows about is one that you would indeed be interested in and qualified for? Then indicate an interest, but do not lose sight that you are not looking for another job, you are looking for an opportunity. If your friend introduces you to the company positioned as a "jobseeker," you are done because you are negotiating for a paycheck. You have fallen into the HR trap and been positioned as someone looking for a paycheck. Do you understand the difference between a job and an opportunity? Do you recognize how important first impressions are to avoid being labeled as a "desperate jobseeker"? Your banner wavers must understand that the issue of positioning your value is paramount to your potential success in any introduction they might make. Emphasize: You are looking for an opportunity, not a job. You are seeking to add measurable value that you can demonstrate and refer to in terms of case studies in other positions you've held that illustrate how you've accomplished the value you propose (see Module Seven: Leaving a Good Footprint).

Method 2: Think and Act Like an Agent Going Direct to Companies

Going back to The Story of You, identify the *key talent* that you possess. Who or what company needs this specific and unique talent? If we were to use a sports agent analogy, take a moment to identify your core strength (best talent) as an athlete. What is it? Be extremely clear, because if you were an agent, everyone knows that you wouldn't call Dayton Moore (General Manager of the Kansas City Royals baseball team) with a shortstop when he needs a catcher. Who needs your unique talent? What kind of company desperately needs what you offer? Think about representing your best talent to the market, just as a sports agent would represent a very specialized form of athlete to the market. If you would like some entertainment and inspiration, watch the movie, Jerry Maguire, which is an entertaining look at the lives and focus required from sports agents.

Ask yourself constantly: Why talk to *any* company that doesn't need what you are best at, which is most likely what you love doing?

Instead of retrofitting yourself into "every job," act like your own agent and *go direct* to companies that need *exactly* what you have to offer. How do you begin to do this? You need to start by thinking like an agent, embracing the attitude and actions of being your own agent. How do agents think? What skills do they need and how do they engage?

An agent does not waste time. He or she is *extremely* focused. This person is only interested in the tightly defined little box of what relates to the story of them.

An agent is not distracted. He or she is very strategic and targeted. He is simply not interested *at all* in anything that *wastes time*. So, why spend your time pursuing one hundred deals that you must retrofit yourself into versus focusing on ten deals that represent legitimate opportunity? We are defining legitimate opportunity as those companies that have a *confirmed* need for what you have identified as your "best talent." In thinking like an agent, it is critical that you focus on quality, not quantity. In acting like an agent, you go direct to people who are *doing what you want to do* or to decision makers in companies that need what you have to offer. Consider positioning yourself as a contract-based employee solution, a full-time employee resource interested in joining the leadership team, or an entrepreneurial service provider that can address a specific need. For any path you choose, there are approaches we describe (and tools and templates associated with this module that you can use to ask for the opportunity) that will help you to accomplish your goals.

Method 3: Establish Relationships That Will Help Confirm Opportunity

While you are focused on industries and companies you want to target because they need your best talent, what's very important is that you zero in on identifying *relationships* that will *bridge your efforts directly into these industries or companies*. Remember always, relationships are everything! How do you find companies (and identify contacts within the companies and or industries) that need your best talent? Here are four channels.

- **Publications and Libraries**: Visit the library and search publications for articles featuring the company and or industry topic of interest. This might be an industry publication, an association publication or general interest article. You want to identify the author of the article (who most likely is a recognized industry expert or thought leader) so that you can reach out to this person by email or phone (whatever you are most comfortable with, but we suggest by phone which is usually listed on the individual's LinkedIn profile). Your goal is to connect with them directly about their article, their insights, and your observation(s) to confirm thoughts or details surrounding an industry or company in specific. How do you begin such a conversation? *Begin by acknowledging them as an industry expert and flatter them. Sincere compliments are an excellent way to establish instant rapport.* Once you connect with them personally, share with them the purpose of the call, which is to ask them about their opinion of the value of your best talent in relation to their impressions of the industry or company, exploring how they would suggest you position this best talent in an effort to make headway into the industry. Approach the subject respectfully and you will be surprised how they may have ideas for you as they have knowledge, relationships and insider perspectives. They can suggest other individual introductions or resources you should consider. Always offer them access to timely research you have done, or insights you have that might provide them newsworthy content they may want to write about in gracious return for their time. This helps to establish a reciprocal relationship, which is always appreciated.

- **Identify people doing what you want to do and go directly to them**. Use LinkedIn to search by industry or title to find people doing what you want to do. You can look at people who were *past employees* of an organization that you want to work for or with, to learn more about the organization and ask them who they would suggest you reach out to within the organization that does the hiring for the role you for which you are interested. Frequently, they also can confirm details surrounding the problem(s) or strategic challenges you think the organization has that you feel uniquely qualified to address via your best talent. Keep in mind that they may or may not be able to confirm your assumption, but most likely whatever they share with you will be more than you knew before, so it will be helpful.

- **You can reach out to people who currently are in the role that you want to pursue** (even if it is in a *new industry with which you have no prior direct experience*). This can be beneficial to your understanding about the company and the industry. It will confirm the value you offer, and what the process is for establishing a relationship with the decision maker. Why approach these people to establish relationships with them? If they are in a role that you want to pursue, they will very often have recruiters directly contacting them about other positions that are open in the industry (and they can often refer you directly to opportunities or recruiters that may be of interest to you). Additionally, we have witnessed that when someone retires, should they have such an established relationship with someone qualified for their role, often they will *refer you directly to the person hiring* when their job becomes available! Contacting people in the role or industry that you want to pursue delivers benefits on so many levels. But at a minimum, they often will introduce you to others who are doing what you would like to do (or groups like associations or LinkedIn discussion groups perhaps you were unaware of), to help you move forward in your effort to learn more about the industry and establish relationships with those doing what you desire to do.

- **Chamber of Commerce, Directors of Membership Services**. Those who work for the chamber of commerce are selling memberships to companies and are privy to updated market knowledge about those companies (often they are aware of company needs). Taking time to visit with those who work for the chamber about companies of interest and people who hold jobs in those companies that you want to establish relationships with can be *priceless.* They can often provide, *at minimum,* confirmation of your observations, and ideally, can make introductions directly to those that you want to meet on your behalf.

- **LinkedIn Key Word Search**. If you search key words associated with the role or industry you are targeting, often LinkedIn will come up with lists of people or companies that fit this criterion in geographic specific areas of interest. For example, "photography services Tulsa" will pull up geographic specific lists that can be helpful if you want to search a specific industry within a given region.

Method 4: Think Like An Entrepreneur

For one moment, forget everything you think you know about entrepreneurs and ponder this: Entrepreneurs really are nothing more than smart problem solvers. They see a problem that they feel uniquely qualified to solve (that they are passionate about and technically have some knowledge about), they craft a solution, and sell the solution to someone that they suspect wants to buy it. They drive demand in their tiny economy of one, selling the value that they can uniquely deliver. This is the fundamental difference between an Artist and an Entrepreneur; one can sell what he creates. *Can you sell your value?* **We believe absolutely you can!** Now, candidly, does the world really need another accountant, attorney, or an architect? No. Let us be honest, it does not.

However, if you talk to an entrepreneur who is opening an accounting firm, there is something about the way in which they want to do business that *convinces them* that people will pay them for their services. They believe that there is demand for what they can uniquely supply! *Have you ever been paid for what you can uniquely supply?* If so, you need to assume that is evidence that, if you were paid even once, you can be paid again. You *simply need to find the buyer,* as it is the one thing that is keeping you from the income options you require. If you offer value (and who doesn't offer value?), *the only reason you are unemployed right now* is that the people or company that needs what you have to offer hasn't met you yet.

Move forward by beginning to realize that you need to "think like an entrepreneur" even if you aren't ready to commit to becoming one. **Entrepreneurs are always doing three things to position their value and sell it.** The following are the behaviors and mindsets to embrace and emulate in order to go direct to people/companies or strategic partners that can pay or partner with you for access to your value.

Research confirms Entrepreneurs are natural:

- **Prospectors:** They meet people and can't wait to tell the "story of them" with excitement, conviction and enthusiasm. They simply LOVE to talk about their company, their vision, their dream, and the *value* that they, their team or company can deliver to the market. Are you like this? Do you have a Prospector mindset? You need one because people can sense your enthusiasm, conviction, and sheer joy in telling the story of you. You need to "think like a Prospector," communicating *at every opportunity* the story of you and your best talent to those who can relate to its value. (Think cocktail parties, cheering at soccer games, attending PTA meetings, church gatherings, *anywhere* you have a chance to personally connect with others.)

- A Prospector mindset looks at *every* personal interaction as a chance to teach, to add value to others, and as a chance to demonstrate value to any qualified person who wants to listen. A prospector mindset is not bound by a "sales call" type of mentality, but rather sees every relational interaction as a chance to build trust, exchange value and sincerely connect with potential decision makers. In organizations, prospectors are often categorized as "sales folks" or business development professionals, as they "hunt for new business" and "farm core customer" accounts. For Entrepreneurs, sales is a most critical core skill, because without it, you are often an isolated technical expert (highly talented, but without a project pipeline). Pure technical experts are too often unable to convert their value into a reliable source of income, because they *lack the capabilities* of the other two required skills, that of prospector and closer. Be intentional with assuming a prospector mindset as it is required to generate leads as you must become urgent and intentional with your time. Your goal is to fill your pipeline with qualified income earning opportunities, which requires you to think like a Prospector. (We will discuss the exact process in greater detail in the next two modules, but for now contemplate what "thinking and acting like a Prospector" means in your life.)

- **Technical Experts**: What is your "best talent" in your warehouse of skills? Most entrepreneurs start with a simple "technical skill" that they can sell or translate into "market value." *What can you sell? Identifying something to sell is the singular difference between someone who is unemployed and an Entrepreneur*. Therefore, at minimum, we ask you think like an Entrepreneur, because you need to recognize the value that you must sell and market.

- In your personal situation, you have been asked to identify your "best talent," in essence the technical skills you are selling as you seek to uncover opportunity. Can you intentionally think and act like a prospector? Entrepreneurs can. In fact, the future of their company depends on their ability to translate these selling skills to others, because if they can't, they can't exit their own venture! They are instead exhausted Rainmakers, only growing organizationally to the level that they can personally sell and service demand. This is a huge problem that cannot be overstated. To move forward, entrepreneurs *intuitively* switch hats from a Prospector mentality to that of a Technical Expert in the sales process. They do this because in conversation with others, they must qualify who needs their skill, best talent, or technical value to position its value and "qualify opportunity."

- Technical experts don't want to talk to everybody but sense an intuitive connection to the person who can appreciate the value of their best talent, *and* identify the individual that has the *authority* to buy it.

- Exactly how does this happen? It occurs when the conversation pivots from the "Prospector" talking about their passion relating to the value of their best talent, to the details associated with technical skills and solutions they offer. The technical expert can describe how their skills *solve a specific problem* or add value to the buyer. Technical experts do not talk extensive details about their best talent unless typically they've come across someone in a conversation who seems to *need* that talent, values this talent, and has the authority to buy it. Technical experts are not engaged in the process of free consulting or quoting a price, rather they position their value, and scope the opportunity to determine if the proposed project or opportunity is a "good fit for both parties." Once the Prospector senses this and they know they are talking with a qualified potential buyer, the technical expert is in mode to "qualify and scope the opportunity" because people always want two things: as much free consulting as you will give them and a price.

- Technical experts recognize the "free consulting and price" trap. In conversation, until they know they are talking to a qualified buyer, they position to protect the investment of their expertise and time as it is valuable! Why give away a solution when you can sell it to a qualified buyer? They naturally address tough technical questions to describe what is unique about their approach, scoping their expertise against a project opportunity, or buyers need. An illustration of this concept is how a contractor you might consider hiring for a home renovation shows up to walk your home, which provides him a detailed scope of your job.

- During the walk through, he tends to explain how he will address the challenges, create value, or solve your construction problems. The Technical Expert can talk project details, associated costs, and options, as well as timeline for the work to be completed. Considering the behaviors and skills of technical experts, often it is the technical expert that actually does the work or delivers the *technical value* associated with the entrepreneurial organization. *In your situation, you are the Technical Expert representing your "best talent" and warehouse of skills. This is true whether you want a full-time job, contract work, or desire to serve as an outside entrepreneurial resource.* When you meet with a recruiter, person conducting an interview, or decision maker hiring your outside expertise, you engage your technical expertise when you demonstrate in conversation your ability to deliver value. You will leverage this value (skills and expertise), and directly refer to it when you address the buyers' notion of what they should pay for this value (which is fair price for your services).

- **Closer**: Once the Technical Expert has qualified and scoped a legitimate opportunity, it is the skills of the Closer that have both the *ability and authority* to close a deal. Entrepreneurs must have this final skill in the sales and relationship development process, or their pipeline never can move forward. This aspect of the sales process is completely discrete and requires behaviors *different* from that of the prospector and technical expert.

- Closers know how, and feel comfortable asking for the order. They know how to structure an agreement and negotiate price and terms. Do you have these skills? Do you feel comfortable asking for the order and closing opportunities? Please stop and really consider this question. To identify and covert opportunity to income, you need to learn, practice, and plan for these skills to be part of the process you regularly engage with to be successful.

This is how Entrepreneurs move forward intuitively. Can you now see that no matter what your path in moving forward, adapting these skills and mindsets can help you? An Entrepreneur's future (much like yours) hinges on becoming very intentional with these efforts and holding themselves accountable to engage, whether the behavior required is their favorite part of the process or not.

Why is this? The answer is simple. An Entrepreneur's pipeline of opportunity must never be ignored! It must be nurtured, and constantly refilled. This is true for your opportunity pipeline as well!

Stop and take a moment to seriously think about each role described above. Take a moment to reflect on how you *feel* about it. Most people have specific thoughts around which of the roles they naturally feel comfortable with and why. Acknowledging this truth, take comfort in knowing that no matter how you feel, the facts are that this is *just a process,* and *with practice*, any of the roles can be mastered. To achieve mastery, what is required is that you become intentional and accountable for practicing each element of the process. Your accountability partners are there to help you reach this place of confidence in these key skills.

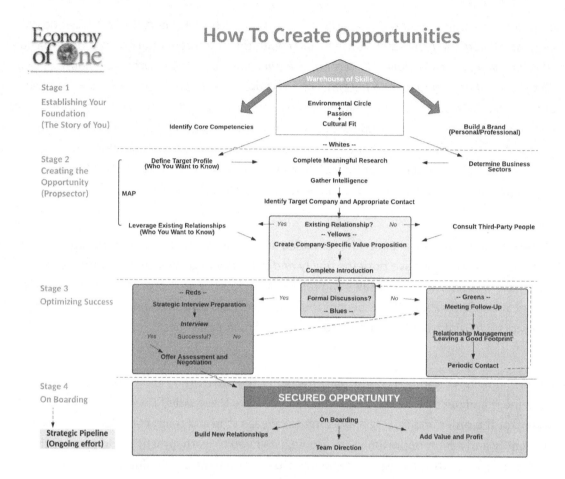

Exercise 1: Your Plan To Uncover Opportunity

Now that you know how many ways there are to engage and move forward, what do you plan to do? Taking action is critical because information is not enough. You must get in the mode of applying what you have learned and practice the process prescribed in order to move forward. It may not feel comfortable, it may feel awkward or intimidating, but you will have support and confidence that you can succeed in "failing forward" *(John Maxwell's book: Failing Forward- Turning Mistakes into Stepping Stones for Success).* What options are best for you? Take a moment to reflect on methods to move forward and pick your top three choices to uncover opportunity. Write these as action items.

Example: I plan to uncover opportunity by going direct to my banner wavers and asking them for introductions to X types of people with these types of job titles in X industry who will appreciate my best talent.

1.
   _____

2.
   _____

3.
   _____

Exercise 2: My Plan To Practice Being A Prospector, Technical Expert, and Closer

1. Which of the three roles am I most comfortable with? Prospector, Technical Expert or Closer? Why is this?

_____

_____

2. Considering my schedule and upcoming commitments, what are upcoming opportunities to practice each role?

_____

_____

3. In which role do I feel I need the most support or practice? Why? Is the challenge an attitude, behavior or under-developed skill?

_____

_____

4. How can my accountability group help me to engage with each role? How can I help them to understand where I am uncomfortable, and what types of ideas will be helpful to me?

_____

_____

5. How can my accountability group help me to practice qualifying an opportunity as a Technical Expert, or engaging techniques to move opportunities to "close"?

_____

_____

6. Moving forward, how can I get intentional, and use my time more effectively to practice and assess my performance with each role?

_____

_____

_____

Next up: You will focus on applying what you have learned in a methodical way. You will develop a detailed MAP (Marketing Action Plan based on relationships you have identified) and YBR (Yellow, Blue, Red) pipeline to manage moving opportunity forward to "close." These two tools and processes are critical to monitor progress and hold yourself accountable. MAP and YBR bring all aspects of the process we have discussed to this point into a succinct method you can easily follow.

Assignments for Next Session

☐ Discuss Module Five with your accountability partners. Address what you feel are your biggest obstacles for success, and brainstorm about how you can practice skills and behaviors to support changes required to address your goals.

☐ Schedule time in your daily calendar to work the strategies to meet others to uncover opportunity.

☐ As you meet with others, be sensitive where they may be struggling. Help them through encouraging suggestions or ideas.

☐ Meet with your accountability partner(s).

☐ Begin acting intentional with the role of Prospector, Technical Expert, and Closer.

☐ Practice "thinking and acting" like an Agent.

☐ Next up, "Start With Your MAP. "

Module Five: Start With Your MAP

Objectives

- How to take inventory of your relationships to systematically uncover opportunities
- How to think about relationships in relation to "revenue"
- How to numerically measure the value of relationships you currently have as they relate to revenue potential
- How to prioritize your short term 30/60/90-day activity plan designed to create, nurture and expand relationships
- How to hold yourself accountable as you make relationships (not network building) a priority
- How to organize and cultivate your relationships with intention on a MAP (Marketing Action Plan)
- How to use Whites on your MAP to identify opportunity, which we label and transfer to a second spreadsheet defined as the YBR (Yellow, Blue, Red). The Yellow, Blue, Red spreadsheet is what you use to track confirmed opportunities, and how to use this spreadsheet is the focus of Module Six

Where Does All Opportunity Come From?

Think about this profound statement for a moment: Most people find almost all of life's opportunities through people they know. How did you meet your significant other? How did you get your first internship or job? Relationships typically are the common denominator. This is why, in searching for opportunity, you need to constantly remind yourself that it's suspected that up to 80% of opportunities are *not posted*. Your MAP© will function as a place for you to start consolidating your entire relationship inventory for the purpose of being very strategic and intentional with your nurture and expansion of these relationships. The word MAP stands for the abbreviation Marketing Action Plan. The MAP, is like a map in that it provides a comprehensive overview of your relational landscape that you can actively navigate and nurture in order to measurably move forward. Most simply described, a MAP is a combined list of who you know and who you want to know.

Track Your Relationships on a MAP

You need to take time to create a MAP. It is simply a list of who you know and who you want to know, so do not let the task of creating it intimidate you. You can accomplish creation of your MAP in a simple excel spreadsheet. If you are overwhelmed with the sheer number of your personal and professional contacts, start with your top 25 relationships and build from here.

Use the MAP to Actively Find Opportunities

How do you convert people to new projects or opportunity? You do it by being intentional with nurturing and expanding your relationships. On your MAP, anyone you know will be referred to as a "white." You will target meeting with as many Whites a week that you can. Why do we call people on the MAP whites? Because out of blank unknowns come opportunity. Consider people a "white blank slate" until you know whether they will be helpful to move forward your efforts. Until you really take the time to get to know these people, and potentially ask for their help, consider them a "blank slate." You will work through meeting with your white relationships to uncover opportunities to pursue and track. The outcome of meeting people is that "projects" will be tracked on a secondary spreadsheet we refer to as your YBR (Yellow, Blue, Red) pipeline. Projects can be a job lead you've heard about, a potential contract or job opening that's coming, a new project associated with a company or person you are qualified to help, or resumes (customized for the opportunity) you have submitted. You will leapfrog from your relationships to the right introductions and referrals to uncover the opportunities you are looking for.

Exercise 1: Start Your MAP

Set up your MAP in Excel or another spreadsheet of your choice. An example of how to set up a MAP is included at the end of this module. The following are prompts to get you thinking about the types of categories of people you ought to focus on.

Take five minutes to add to your initial banner wavers contacts list that you began in Module Three, Networks Versus Relationships:

- People you already know (these can be an extension of the list of Banner Wavers you have already identified) -- keep going and build out the list to a minimum of 25 names
- Groups you belong to or have been connected to in the past (for example college fraternity, sorority, my church, workers from my old company, my wife's dinner group, volunteer groups I've been active in, the PTA, associations I'm active in, etc.)

Now, add people you do not know but *want* to know:

- Hiring managers or employees at companies you want to work for, people who are doing what you want to do, thought leaders in industries you are tracking, and Chamber of Commerce contacts
- Companies (and titles of people) who might need your skills or could introduce you to potentiall clients, people who work in industries or companies you would like to work for

From Relationship to Opportunity

Many times, your best introductions will *not* come from your close friends. Instead, they will come from your banner wavers who run in different circles, as quite simply, they know people you do not.

Expand Your MAP

Your assignment this week is to build out your MAP with greater details. List who you know from sources like:

- Address book, email contacts and social networks (and your significant other's)
- People in groups you have been part of

List who you want to know, including:

- Types of jobs similar to your ideal opportunity
- Companies employing those in titles you are interested in
- People who work there (use social media and company websites to identify them)
- If freelancing, potential sources of clients
- People your banner wavers suggest

Approach the first list (who you know) to introduce you to the second list (who you want to know).

Example: MAP → YBR → Job Offer

Exercise 2: Approach a Contact

Two volunteers, act out Fred and Joe:

- *Fred:* "How's your job search going?"
- *Joe:* "Well, I'm looking for an opportunity, Fred, not a job. I'm wanting to position myself and my value as an entry-level engineer, possibly at EZ Build. I remember you used to work there. Would you happen to know Tim Davis, who is familiar with their engineering needs, or someone else at the company who might be a good person to visit with?"
- *Fred:* "Not a chance! Everyone I knew there has moved on. But if you really want an opportunity as an engineer, why not consider Falco Company? My friend Bob, who is retiring, might recommend you for his old job, and I'd be pleased to introduce you…"
- *Joe:* "Really?"

Hint: Approach people one-to-one (not ever via impersonal mass email).

"Will People Really Help Me?"

Yes, with the right approach:

- People generally *want* to help. Don't you like to help others?
- Flatter them and thank them up front for a few minutes of their time to ask a few questions
- Use your story of you and best talent to help others position your value
- Make it easy and be specific! (Example: "Do you know anyone who works at Speedyboat, Inc.?")

"What If I'm Shy?"

One introvert had only five contacts to put on her MAP. She realized she was really limiting her career! *"So, I got out of my comfort zone. I started meeting people… and that's how I found my next opportunity!"*

Smart Networking

When expanding your relationship base, optimize your time. Do not attend every networking event out there. Target three to five coffees with individuals you know a week, that way you begin talking with people who already know you. Get actively involved. Focus on the quality of your relationships.

Exercise 3: Find an Opportunity

Today, make it your goal to identify one person with a connection to a company that employs people in your industry, or in positions related to your perfect opportunity.

"Does This Really Work?"

Yes, when you do it in an organized, systematic way. Seventy-five percent of Americans work for small and mid-size businesses you have never heard of. Use relationships to find the 80% of hidden jobs and meet the managers before they post it. *You need to be* the reason the job never posts!

Expand Your MAP

Put *everyone* you know on your MAP. All relationships matter. Most people have many more friends and allies than they realize. It is about "Yes, I like you and trust you" vs. "No, it is not a good match and most likely you won't help me."

Group your contacts and follow the ranking system below:

- Premium contacts (4 or 5 ratings)—well-connected, insightful or most likely to help if asked
- Past professional contacts (1-3 ratings)—colleagues, vendors and providers
- Online or offline contacts (rate accordingly)—networking groups, other peers and social media sites
- Professional association contacts (rate accordingly)
- Personal contacts (rate accordingly)—childhood friends and people from hobby, faith, or university groups

- Friends and family (rate accordingly)—especially those who have professional networks of their own

Rank your contacts from Ones to Fives:
1. They do not know me
2. They know me but have never helped me
3. They know me and have helped on occasion
4. They are a trusted advocate
5. They are trusted and have demonstrated they will actively help by sending me referrals and making introductions

Basic Sample MAP:

Rank	People I Know	From...	Contact Info	Notes, next steps
5 – Banner Waver	Sara Little	SaSa, Inc.	sl@sasa.com	I need to thank Sara for the introduction to Frank by 10-12
5- Banner Waver	Paul Perry	College	perry@uni.edu	Paul's uncle holds a position in an industry I'd like to know more about, ask for intro by 10-15
5- Banner Waver	Stan Lind	College	555.6588	Dept Head: Will ask for industry intros in consulting finance by 10-15
4	Paul Efrain	Classmate	pe@gmail.com	Classmate in MIS 320, need to reconnect by 10-20
3	Steve Walt	Classmate	walt@com.net	Fellow intern at SaSa, reconnect by 10-20
2	Tom White	EZRecs	555.6541	Ask Paul for intro to Tom. Think they need my best talent by 10-15
1		Emerald Co	od@em.com	No contact, use LI to identify past employee doing what I want to do by 10-15

MAP Sample

Rank	Help Level
1	Don't Know
2	Know But Never Helped
3	Helped
4	Loyal and Dependable
5	Sends Intros and Referrals

PLC	Premium Level Contacts	People I Know: Decision Makers, Influential, etc.
BW	Banner Wavers	Colleagues, People I trust to ask for help
PC	Personal Contacts	From School, Church, Clubs - focus on who I know and need to know
NG	Networking Groups	People in networking groups I need to update or get to know better
IE	Industry Expert	Targeting to confirm info on companies of interest or industry intel
PAC	Professional Association Contacts	People I know from professional workgroups or associations
FF	Family and Friends	Providing an update on companies I'm targeting, skills I'm developing, ideas I'm pursuing
COE	Calendar of Events	Update my schedule to reflect events I want to attend

Help Level	Contact Type	First Name	Last Name	E-mail Address	Phone Number	Company	Comments
5	BW	Bill	Allen	Bill.Allen@kc.rr.com	(913) 555-8888	Acme, Inc.	Ask intro to Bill
5	BW	Don	Smith	Don.Smith@gmail.com	(505) 123-4567	Marketsmartz	Meet Sprint contact
5	BW	Mary	Brown	Mary.Brown@aol.com	(913) 210-8765	Code	Ask for intros- telcos
5	BW	Sue	Jones	Sue.Jones@bozo.com	(816) 777-6664	ABC Co	Recruiter, met at job fair
5	BW	Allie	Morgan	Allie.Morgan@comcast.com	(913) 456-7890	All Hands on Deck	Ask to meet frat brothers
5	BW	Scott	Simpson	Scott.Simpson@bingo.com	(913) 555-8888	EA Enterprises	Ask to meet brother in law
4	NG	Dean	Gilbert	Dean.Gilbert@marketsmartz.com	(505 123-4567	Acme, Inc.	Meet friend at Pepsi.
4	NG	Fred	Copeland	Fred.Copeland@code.com	(913) 210-8765	Marketsmartz	Aunt Sally's brother in law
4	PPC	Ed	Johnson	Ed.Johnson@kc.rr.com	(816) 777-6664	Code	Ask about CGI
4	FF	Tom	Wilson	Tom.Wilson@gmail.com	(913) 456-7890	ABC Co	met thru LinkedIn
4	PLC	Sally	Williams	Sally.Williams@aol.com	(913) 555-8888	All Hands on Deck	Request meeting
4	PC	Bev	Allen	Bev.Allen@bozo.com	(505) 123-4567	EA Enterprises	Recruiter, met at NLJC job fair
3	PC	Deb	Smith	Deb.Smith@comcast.com	(913) 210-8765	Acme, Inc.	Send article, nurture
3	PPC	Bill	Brown	Bill.Brown@bingo.com	(816) 777-6664	Marketsmartz	Send blog, expand
3	NG	Don	Jones	Don.Jones@marketsmartz.com	(913) 456-7890	Code	Ask about value prop
3	PC	Mary	Morgan	Mary.Morgan@code.com	(913) 555-8888	Economy of One	HR Telecom
3	PC	Sue	Simpson	Sue.Simpson@kc.rr.com	(505) 123-4567	All Hands on Deck	Meet her boss
2	IE	Allie	Gilbert	Allie.Gilbert@gmail.com	(913) 210-8765	EA Enterprises	Ask about Apple
2	IE	Scott	Copeland	Scott.Copeland@aol.com	(816) 777-6664	Acme, Inc.	Send thank you for info
2	NG	Dean	Johnson	Dean.Johnson@bozo.com	(913) 456-7890	Marketsmartz	met thru LinkedIn
1	FF	Sally	Smith	Sally.Smith@code.com	(816) 777-6664	EA Enterprises	met thru LinkedIn
1	PC	Bev	Brown	Bev.Brown@kc.rr.com	(913) 456-7890	Acme, Inc.	Tell story of me
1	PC	Sue	Allen	Sue.Allen@code.com	(913) 555-8888	Marketsmartz	Send industry article
1	PPC	Allie	Smith	Allie.Aim@marketsmartz.com	(505) 123-4567	Code	Ask for coffee

From Relationship To Purpose

Relationships add meaning of life. Your purpose is not just *what* you do, but *who* you do it with! What does your MAP tell you about the *quality* of relationships you currently have? Is it obvious you might really have some work to do and have not been as focused on truly nurturing relationships? If so, do not feel bad as this is often the case when people begin this process. Comfort yourself in knowing that this is a starting place and a process that is something you work on for life, so take things one day at a time, and do not get overwhelmed.

Managing Your Whites On Your MAP: 30/60/90 Day Plan

When a contact either moves up in rank or drops in rank (after you ask for help), then you need to update your spreadsheet and re-prioritize accordingly. When planning use of your time, the first 30 days, assuming you have a healthy list, you want to focus on #4's and #5's. Day 30 to 60 focuses on #3's, #2's then #1's. Keep in mind that if one of your #5 Banner Wavers introduces you to a #1, then following up with a direct introduction takes priority. The idea is that you begin with people you know well, gain confidence in your communication process, then expand your reach, slowly moving from "farming core relationships" to "hunting for new ones."

The ranking system makes it possible to truly track your progress as your goals are to maintain #4's and #5's in the first 30 days, asking for help and thanking them for help in telling the story of you to their relational base. Days 31-60 you need to expand this core and take it to new relational outreach, focusing perhaps on your #2's and #3's. By day 60-90 you need to really have worked the core of your existing network and be rapidly expanding your relational base with focused strategy and intention. You need to keep this tight focus working on a 30/60/90-day plan because you need to see true and measurable progress. Too often, depending on the timeframe of your transition, it is too easy not to focus or become urgent and intentional with your work. Do not think this way. Every day, you are spending your time (money) on things. Ask yourself: Is it producing the results you want? To illustrate this point, one participant in our workshop really struggled with depression and lethargy, while simultaneously becoming very anxious about her unemployment running out. Updating your MAP takes a bit of time as you work through weekly priorities, but it is critical to stay organized and know where you are in the process. In the note section, no more than a few notes should be included (do not write a bunch of information). What should be the focus of your notes is the next step and a due date for the next step to be completed. A fourth grader ought to be able to read it and understand what "next step" is required.

Accountability Meeting Agenda

:00 Review

- ☐ Major events, use of time and volunteer work
- ☐ Are you hitting a 70/30 mix in terms of use of your time? 70% focus on Banner Wavers, 30% on volunteer work that is meaningful to you. If not, why?
- ☐ Homework (review the Story of You, your best talent, and plan to contact five people on your calendar in the next week)

:15 Discuss

- ☐ Your current MAP
- ☐ Plans to expand and improve your MAP

:35 Homework

- ☐ Expand your MAP: What areas or segments will you focus on (who you know vs. who you want to know)? How do your plans relate to thinking like an Agent, Headhunter, Connector and Recruiter? How do your priorities reflect your goals to bridge into relationships that will connect you with people who will be helpful?
- ☐ Deadline: By when will your top 25 be complete and ranked? When will you begin farming? Hunting?
- ☐ How will you score success and focus your efforts in first 30 days, 60 days, 90 days?
- ☐ Contact five people to begin the relationship building and nurturing process. Have a strategy of how each meeting with each person can bridge you to industries or people you would like to speak with or ask for an introduction to.
- ☐ Deadlines?
- ☐ How will you score and measure success? How will your ratings of people on your MAP change from the initial rating effort and adjust over time?

:55 Scoring and Closing Encouragement

- ☐ Review progress with your efforts from this past week
- ☐ End with encouragement and observations about how you sense your approach to identifying opportunity might be changing. How do you feel about your sense of progress and organization?

Assignments

- ☐ Read and do exercises in Module Six: The YBR
- ☐ Meet with your accountability partner(s)
- ☐ Continue improving your MAP
- ☐ Contact five Whites (people) appropriate to uncover opportunities
- ☐ Set up a secondary spreadsheet outside of your MAP of people. You will use this and refer to it in the next module as your YBR

Module Six: The YBR

MAP
Approach
Prospect Pool

Follow Up Post-
Sale, Greens
Get Referrals

Generate
Yellow Leads
Prospector

Sales Pitch, Red Leads
In-Person Interview
Closer

Qualify Blue Leads
Initial Interview
Technical Expert

Objectives

By the end of this module you will know:

- The definition of "YBR Spreadsheet" and how to use it in relation to your MAP
- How to approach White contacts (Banner Wavers and their networks, as well as other relationships you identify and prioritize) on your MAP to uncover opportunities
- Understand the definitions of Yellow, Blue, Red and Green as they relate to your opportunity pipeline
- How to move an opportunity from one phase of qualification to another (from Yellow classification to Blue, from Blue to Red, from Red to Green, then re-cycle the relationship to renew again on your MAP)
- That this is just a "process" with "yes and no" outcomes: You will be empowered to understand how to leverage this process to your vantage and begin practicing attitudes, skills and behaviors important to each color classification
- How to interpret results on your YBR, being able to adjust appropriately to maximize outcomes
- That this is a life-long process, not a short-term solution to connect to your next paycheck

Your next opportunity is hidden with a connection on your MAP! Ready to find it?

What Is the YBR? How Do I Use It?

Simply, the YBR is a color-coded spreadsheet that you use to track opportunities that are uncovered by having discussions with people listed on your MAP. It is a color-coded pipeline that will guide you in evaluating next steps and monitoring your progress. While the MAP and YBR are both essentially spreadsheets, each one serves a very distinct purpose. Do not confuse this detail as it is critical. The MAP is a list of <u>people</u> you know and want to know. The YBR is a list of <u>opportunities (or projects)</u> that you have generated from conversations with others. On the YBR, there are simple color definitions that indicate where an opportunity you are tracking is at in terms of stage of development. Why add color? Research suggests that adult learning and retention goes up 80% when color is applied.

Yellow: This is a specific opportunity you have identified in acting like a Prospector. It is associated with a person within a company, and is something that is going to happen, just not right now. This person has indicated that the company will be doing "something" that is a fit with your interests, but it will happen sometime <u>in the future</u>. <u>It is a confirmed opportunity (they have it in the budget or in the production timeline or strategic plan), it is not a wishful guess or a hope</u>. A person has confirmed a definite project, an employment or some type of contract opening, some type upcoming opportunity, or something of interest (upcoming job posting). For whatever reason, they just are not in position to move on it just yet. These are "golden" yellow opportunities because often they exist in the minds or sphere of influence of people who happen to know about them. They are not necessarily known in the public domain. Yellows tend to be based on inside information, which means you have a strong opportunity to position yourself as a unique resource without the added pressure of mass competition. You have time with Yellows to develop the relationship, to explore their needs (as a Technical Expert) and position your value in order to qualify if the opportunity is a good fit. Typically, a Prospector mindset is what generates the Yellow opportunity. You are talking to people, and enjoying building a quality relationship with them when they mention something about the industry, about one of their contacts, or about an upcoming trigger event that would open the door for you to provide specific value. To generate a Yellow, you need to be engaged with others, confident about your value, and listening very carefully to what they are telling you (not just focused on the Story of You).

Blue: This too is a specific opportunity associated with a person within a company, but the difference is that they are willing to <u>meet now with you to discuss the opportunity in detail</u>. When this happens, you are switching from a Prospector mentality to that of a Technical Expert. The difference between classification of a Yellow and a Blue is that in a Yellow meeting the contact is describing *something that will happen sometime in the future*. In a Blue meeting, *you are actively engaged in qualifying an opportunity that is happening now*. In practical terms, you might meet with a White from your MAP, and in an initial conversation with them, they identify an opportunity and want to discuss it in detail. The first meeting in essence moves from a Yellow to a Blue. While in "Blue" meetings, the mindset required is that you intentionally "cool off." Sounds counter intuitive? It is! While you may be thinking to yourself "sell, sell, sell," and get all excited at an opportunity, the mindset required to manage a Blue meeting is to *intentionally cool off* and think very rationally about the opportunity at hand. In Blue meetings:

- You want to slow down to make sure that you indeed are a good fit for what the person or company is describing
- You are positioning the value of your best talent from your warehouse of skills (not just providing free consulting and a price)
- You are asking them about their level of experience with such a project, position, or consulting solution in the past. From this you are determining if they've ever bought a solution like the one you can offer, or you are factoring in an education curve (to educate them on the value of what you can offer in relation to the price you would charge). Either way, your challenge in blue meetings is to scope the work, project or opportunity at hand. In a blue meeting you are gathering the information you need to estimate the work, project or opportunity you want to compete for.

A Blue opportunity may encompass one meeting (hearing the scope of the job, project or opportunity), or may require a number of meetings where essentially you are meeting to estimate the value of what it is you can provide, matching it against the needs of the company. You may meet with one individual or several people involved in the process. In traditional job seeking, Blue meetings are when you have identified a specific opportunity (a Yellow), and now you are meeting to discuss your qualifications via a phone or face-to-face interview. Throughout the process of managing a Blue, you are trying to understand in depth exactly what value you must create to meet the decision makers "definition of success." You might be asking about other service providers they have had, other employees they have hired, or just their experience in trying to get their need met. All of this information will arm you in how to position the value of your solution and provide you the input you need to create compelling case studies for "why you."

Red: Once a Blue has indicated a request for a proposal, or desire for a customized resume, the Blue is reclassified and transfers to a Red. The mindset and behaviors of the Technical Expert shift to the mindset and skills associated with that of a Closer. Criteria for an opportunity that is classified as Red, are that there is a <u>definite opportunity</u> or project of interest, they are <u>actively meeting</u> with people to discuss it, <u>and</u> they've requested that you <u>propose a solution or submit a customized resume</u> (whether you are applying for contract work, a full time position, or if they are reviewing you as a consulting entrepreneurial resource). Reds are "red hot" as often they are moving fast, do have known competition, and require <u>immediate attention</u> or action to position for consideration. Closers seek to answer 8 questions. These include:

- What is the definitive timeline for the project, hire or opportunity? Is the financing and budget in place?
- Have I met and spent time with the decision maker(s)?
- Do I know the decision-making criteria that will be used to review my proposal, measure my value or review the hire?
- Who/What is the competition?

- Have I addressed the proprietary nature of the solution I can provide? Have I provided plenty of illustrations of the value of my solution, and how it specifically meets their needs and definition of success?
- What are their assumptions about price as it relates to their definition of value?
- What is the timeline for a decision to be made once a proposal, a resume, or bio is submitted?
- What is the agenda for the next meeting? What are the next steps to move this to close? Should I keep this opportunity in my pipeline, or is it time to remove it? (As a Closer, you have the power to determine next steps.)

Green: Once a Red has made a "yes or no" decision on your proposal, resume, or bio then the key relationship or person associated with the Red opportunity is re-classified as a Green. Greens are relationships that have made a yes or no decision and they are evergreen. They can be recycled and rotate back to your MAP. If you have done a proper job in building the relationship, on stating and positioning your value, and on asking for the business, then often even if they don't select you for the particular opportunity you are pursuing, they may call you back on the next opportunity that you are a fit for. This is especially true if you are engaged in "post sales" relationship building where you follow up further after they've filled the project or position, just to "see how things are going," and check in with them. We have witnessed often that the hire does not work out, or there is some unforeseen issue, that then opens the door to even further opportunities, which is why all relationships are evergreen. They need to be nurtured past a yes or decision, because by this time the person you've invested time with, now knows you (likes you and trusts you), which is the required prerequisite to doing business! While they may not be a fit, often they will refer you on to others who they may know of that might be a good fit. Never forget the value of <u>evergreen</u> relationships! Once past decision, a Green is transferred back onto the MAP for continued nurturing, unless you determine after having proposed a solution that culturally an ongoing relationship with the individual is a poor fit.

Organizing Your MAP: Whites and 30/60/90 Day Priorities

Every week, if you are in full-time transition, you should be approaching a minimum of five people to expand and nurture your relationships. Initially these are Banner Wavers, and those that you feel confident can repeat the Story of You, and properly position you (not as a Desperate Jobseeker, but as a true resource). These initial people you know well are reaching out to others in their networks. They are categorized as Whites, and you are farming these (nurturing them) to sow value with them, and hopefully reap a crop of opportunity. From "White" or a "blank slate" of relationships emerge Yellow, Blue or Red opportunity.

As you gain confidence in the farming process (the first 30 days typically) you will begin to "hunt," going outside core existing relationships to new relationships in days 60-90. Keep in mind, this is recommended in an ideal world. *We completely realize that your world might not be ideal.* If this is the case, it is okay. From day one, if you choose to engage in both farming and hunting behavior there is no problem with this, except that you need to be *very mindful* of the learning curve. You need to identify with the aid of your accountability group what is working, and not working as you make progress, not losing sight of the fact that this is a process that does have a learning curve. With the luxury of time you can focus on intentional practice, moving from the shallow end of the swimming pool (farming) to the deep end (hunting).

Tools you are using include transcripts, email templates (please see all included to this point), and personal appeals for help. The key to your effort is to position yourself effectively as a personal and professional resource to everyone you interact with, avoiding the label of "desperate jobseeker" at every turn.

The YBR also serves as a diagnostic tool to examine what is working well in your personal progress, and what is not.

Exercise 1: Choose Five Whites

Look at your MAP and choose five people you already know who are most likely to:
- Introduce you to a person you want to know
- Or, lead to an unknown opportunity

1.
_____
2.
_____
3.
_____
4.
_____
5.
_____

With a partner, talk about who you chose:
- Why do you think these five people are most likely to give you a helpful introduction? In talking with these 5, are you farming existing relationships or hunting?
- Who are you ultimately aiming to reach on your list of people you want to know? (You could be aiming to reach a type of person by title, or within a specific industry, instead of a specific name, unless you have been provided one.)

Your Role as a Prospector

In your approach, spark interest in what you have to offer. You are *prospecting* for opportunities. Remember, you are positioning your value to people—not companies! Mention that you are building your network of relationships, and most likely in position to meet their next employee, contractor or client. You have a tremendous value to offer them when they invest time, they just need to recognize it.

Prospecting: A Habit for Life

Not every White will know of an opportunity right now. Cultivate the relationship anyway. Even, or especially when, you have a job! You never know how you might be able to help each other later.

Your Role as a Prospector

Prospectors get hired. Why? Because every business feels the pressure to find and retain new customers. Employers crave rainmakers and find it very hard to fire them as they cultivate relationships that are often measured by revenue.

Suggested Approach to Whites

- Initial Email (direct, open and specific ask). Warning: Do not send mass email to all
- Offer specific times to meet or call
- Meet
- Follow-up and Thank you

Before you call, send a friendly email. Ask to talk. Say directly and openly exactly what you want to talk about. (Example: "I'm looking for work as a software engineer and I'm targeting Acme, Inc. I can see through LinkedIn that you know a past employee. Might we talk for a few minutes on Friday?")

When you write them a note ahead of time, you:
- Arrange to talk at a time convenient for them
- Give them a chance to think of who they might know, instead of just getting an off-the-cuff, rushed response
- Avoid awkward, unexpected requests

If you meet in person (vs. on the phone), you are likely to get a good result. A safe amount of time to ask for is 30 minutes.

If they cannot meet with you until a time more than a week away, send them a reminder email the day before.
- Example: "John, I'm really looking forward to connecting with you tomorrow. Are we still on for 2pm at Joe's Coffee House?"

Prepare for the Meeting

If you did a good job in your opening email, your prospect should expect you:
- To arrive with a proposed agenda, and possibly a bio or summary of the story of you
- To ask for help meeting specific people you already mentioned in your email
- To follow up later on specific action points

Sample Meeting Agenda

Meeting with Mike Strouse, May 12

- Overview of bio and goals in identifying "next opportunity"
- Possible connections at Acme, or in industries, and titles or names of people of interest (people doing what you want to do)
- John Newhouse, Mark Robbins, Mia Chao
- Ask about people working in target department
- Other targets: TS Inc, Lott LLC, Paul Mills + ?
- Any connections/favors/resources I can offer Mike?
- Next step is to follow up on commitments to Mike and updates to him on my progress with his suggestions

What Not to Do

Bemoan your terrible situation and desperately beg for a JOB or paycheck. Begging is obvious, painful and puts the other person in an immediately awkward position.

You want their most trusted relationships. Who would *you* give such access? What type of person would a person need to be for you to provide such trust?

During the Meeting

- Ask about their lives, who they are as a person, and how they are doing
- Ask them about their path within the industry, and why they enjoy doing what they do (see what you can learn from them)
- Be positive, sensitive to the clock, and sincerely thank them for their time

Afterwards, write them a thank-you note and express a desire to return the favor.

Exercise 2: Practice Your Approach

- Write your initial email to one of your chosen Whites
- Share it with a partner (playing the role of your White)
- Have a mock meeting
- Ask for constructive feedback from your accountability partner

Remember: Most People Will Want to Help You

Making an introduction feels good! And, if you prove valuable to their contact, it increases their social currency.

Push Past the Fear of Asking for Help

Your brain has two modes. Neurologists call these modes *sympathetic* and *parasympathetic.* You call them *fight-or-flight* and *relaxed*.

- Example: "Oh no, it's a bear!" How will you react? (Wild bear vs. Teddy bear).

- Example: "Oh no, he's calling my college buddy!" (To ask about opportunities vs. to chat about the ballgame)
- Remember yourself in your most confident life or job moment. This is when you were happiest or most content. Practice this mindset! Use and resort to this mindset in preparation to meet with others, or to reach out by phone.

Exercise 3: Set Up An Initial YBR, What Does It Tell You?

Use the second Excel spreadsheet you set up when you set up your MAP. Enter the following headers:

- Name of Project/Job/Opportunity:
- Key Contact:
- 8 Question Answers:
- Next Action:
- Notes:

Once done with headers, add all the projects/ proposals or jobs that you are pursuing right now. Think very carefully about the yellow, blue and red color code definitions. Apply these colors over the otherwise White spreadsheet you are working from. What does the distribution of the colors tell you about yourself? Is there a large number of Yellows but few blues? How old are your call-back dates under the next action column? Are you a strong Prospector, but struggle to qualify opportunity in the Blue, or convert Blues in the mindset of a closer to request a proposal, thus moving the opportunity to red? In an *ideal* pipeline there is three times the numbers of Yellows to two times the number of total Blues to Reds. Many Yellows create "gold" in the pipeline. Few Blues or a "Blue hole" indicates that perhaps you have a tough time moving from Prospector to a Technical Expert (qualify the opportunity) mentality. A preponderance of reds may indicate you are chasing anything that moves, are competing on price, or are not really qualifying the opportunity before you make a proposal or submit a resume. The beauty of the color codes is that it offers a specific diagnostic tool to help you focus on next step attitudes and behaviors required to move an opportunity forward. It also reveals productivity. Provided you have the time, every week you should meet with five Whites, with hope you identify two Yellows, and perhaps a Blue or Red. These are realistic productivity goals.

Sample YBR

Color	Opportunity Name	Contact Name	Email	How I Found	Next Action	Results	Next Action or Call Back	Anticipated Start
Red	Contract Work@ Sprint	Debbie Mae	dmae@sprint.com	Intro from Bill Moss	Send Thank You w/ case studies of value	Debbie wants me to meet her department managers	02/03	4/22
Red	Full-Time Internship	Frank Meyer	Fmeyer@abc.com	Intro Sue Klein	Send portfolio	Skype Interview	01/23	Summer
Blue	Full time Internship	Bob Sands	Bsands@Bizco.com	Professor Blake Recommendation	Find out if my skills are a fit	Fill out online application	01/04	Summer
Blue	Project with Bank Marketing Dept	Mary Kate, Regional Director	Mkate@ABS.com	Intro from Bob Sheldon	Ask about hourly fee rate	Submit proposal for work / scope of project	Due 5/14	?
Yellow	Part-Time Work	Sara Treanor	Streanor@mac.com	My Dad knows Bob Felding, President	Who is the decision maker?	Learned their definition of success	04/02	?
Yellow	New Position, Maggie Moos Marketing Dept	David Frank	Dfrank@Moo.com	Recommended by Mom's friend, Allison	Thank Allison. Find out scope of work	Send customized letter of value to David Frank, ask to meet him for portfolio review	?	?
White	Informational Interview	Dorrie Clark	Dclark@Acme.com	Industry Expert	Send her detailed thank you	Also, nurture this relationship and expand. Send to her any research that might interest her.	01/12	

Exercise 4: Freedom From Fear

Take five minutes and explore your biggest fear about approaching Whites on your MAP, and in moving YBR's forward. List your thoughts, emotions, and likely behaviors if you listen to this fear. What lie does this fear tell you about who you are?

Thoughts on Whites: (Example: "No one will help me. Why should they?")

_____

_____

Emotions: (Examples: "ashamed, afraid, vulnerable")

_____

_____

Behaviors: (Examples: "avoid calling, apologize for calling, looking down [no eye contact]")

_____

_____

_____

Root Lie: (Example: "I am not worth their time.")

_____

_____

_____

Below the root lie, write its opposite—the truth—that affirms who you are:

Truth: (Example: "I am worthy of their friendship, time and professional partnership.")

_____

_____

_____

If you believe this, how will you feel? Think? Act?

_____

_____

_____

As you think about the role of Prospector, Technical Expert, and Closer, what does your current YBR tell you about your respective personal strengths or weaknesses as they relate to these three roles and distribution of color on your initial YBR? How can your accountability group help you to change behaviors to address a lack of Yellows, Blues and Reds?

_____

_____

_____

Forces That Work Against You

For discussion with your accountability partners: What will keep you from calling Whites?

- Fear
- Resistance to Change
- Call reluctance

Your weapon against these obstacles? Personal choice and practice. When you are nervous about reaching out to others, take time and think about when people ask you for your help. Do you slam the phone down and get rude, or do you generally take the call and be kind? Research suggests that most people, when asked for help, will kindly offer it.

Choose to Make a Change

The alternative is to think, "What if I don't change at all and something magical just happens?" This isn't realistic and enables otherwise unproductive behavior.

What is Resistance to Change?

We repeat the same thoughts, emotions and behaviors... no matter what our circumstances. We do it because it feels comfortable. This can become a *stagnant stronghold* in your thinking, and how you think leads to the root of how you behave and attitudes you harbor.

Why Are We Resistant to Change?

The brain learns routine and feels relaxed when we do what is familiar. We stay in our comfort zones because we are afraid of the unknown. You need to ask and discuss in your accountability groups: "What could happen if I change? What are the risks, potential rewards?" You need to make note of attitudes that need to change, behaviors that need adjustment, or skills that you should further develop.

Choice Creates the New Familiar

The more Whites you contact, the more familiar it will feel, and the more relaxed you will be. Choose to make a change and start authentically connecting with people.

Accountability Meeting Agenda

:00 Review

- [ ] Major events: each person chooses highlights that illustrate progress
- [ ] Homework review and update your YBR. What does it indicate to you about the health of your opportunity pipeline?

:15 Discuss

- [ ] What you have learned so far in your approach to White contacts?
- [ ] Who did you approach and how? What worked or did not work?
- [ ] Role-play your approach as a Prospector, Technical Expert and Closer. Get feedback from your accountability partners about your strengths, weaknesses and areas for growth or expansion of skills

:35 Homework

- [ ] Schedule next steps for YBR opportunities
- [ ] Review what you know today about the 8 questions and Blue opportunities
- [ ] Deadlines, next steps and call back dates?
- [ ] How you will measure success this week?
- [ ] Goals
- [ ] How will I focus on becoming more aware of my attitudes and behaviors throughout the week? What is working and what is not?

:55 Scoring and Closing Encouragement

- [ ] Update your efforts from this past week in terms of new Yellows, Blues, Reds or Greens
- [ ] End with encouragement, and identify and discuss one thing about each person in the accountability group that is noticeably improving

Assignments for Next Session:

- [ ] Continue to build YBR and make progress with your MAP
- [ ] Read Module Seven: Leaving A Good Footprint
- [ ] Meet with your accountability partner

Module Seven: Leaving A Good Footprint

Objectives

By the end of this module, you will know:

- How to stay very aware of attitudes and behaviors that lead to "retrofitting yourself" into a company culture that isn't a good fit
- How to identify and value the "x factor" when interviewing a company or person
- How to create meaningful documentation that "leaves behind a good footprint" (something that can lead people uniquely back to you) with every single person you meet, at every interaction
- How to write a "thank you note on steroids"
- How to author addendums to any meeting that effectively convey details of (exactly) how you create measurable value based on experiences you've had, and challenges overcome (customized case studies)
- What kills a "good footprint"
- The role your human brand plays in the process
- How to nurture relationships over the phone by leaving great voicemails
- How to think like a Technical Expert and Closer as you qualify each opportunity in your pipeline
- How to properly position opportunity to "close" and ask for the opportunity or business

Eye On Corporate Culture: Is The Opportunity A True Fit?

Looking back at the YBR, when you follow up with a yellow that indicates an opportunity is now active and it's appropriate to meet, the yellow is re-categorized as a blue. In blue meeting interactions, your goal is to "cool down" and think *very rationally* about the opportunity at hand. In preparation, you want to review your story of you, and revisit your "perfect opportunity" description that was an exercise in Module Two. You want to reference these and keep them in front of you as you determine "if the opportunity I'm preparing to meet, that is now a blue in my pipeline, is a good fit for me." *Just because you have an opportunity presenting does not mean it is a solid fit for you.* Clearly, if what you wrote as a "perfect opportunity" does not come close to matching the opportunity you are reviewing, you need to ask yourself why. Typical reasons why include:

-**Pressure to just get a job or a "paycheck."** For whatever reason, your transition is dragging out and there's strong financial or significant other pressure to just "do something" (the anything is better than nothing mentality).

-You are encountering many possibilities and not wanting to miss anything, you find yourself responding to everything. Yet are still not making the progress you'd hoped.

-You review virtually every job description with a mindset to fit yourself into the description you are reading. If what HR says is that they need "X," you want to present "X," because this is what they say they need, not because you *think of yourself* in these terms. This mindset is *particularly dangerous* in that you are squarely positioning yourself as a *desperate jobseeker*. You subtly indicate that you are willing to morph into anything HR says, the decision maker says, or the recruiter says they need to "get the job" and fit the description.

Any of these scenarios are unproductive and frustrate your efforts. If you are "faking it to make it," be aware that it is a matter of time until you are discovered. You simply can't fake who you are as a person, *nor should you*. Think of a company for a moment as a personality type. Each department is led by people who constitute a different attribute of what could be considered an organizational "personality." Since organizations are comprised of people, it's natural that companies take on personality attributes similar to people in terms of culture. When you think about a company's culture, you need to compare the "fit" of this culture to your own personal style. This is true no matter what type of opportunity you may be exploring (contractor, full time / part time employee, or entrepreneurial resource). You need to ask:

Do I see myself fitting in with the team I'm assigned to work with?

Do I relate to the organization's business challenges?

Does it energize me to think about my role in providing solutions? Or, does the thought of doing what they say they need me to do leave me feeling bored or unexcited (without emotional response)?

Am I comfortable with the politics I sense are ingrained in the organizational culture?

How do I feel about the office "work vibe," religious, or political viewpoints of leadership?

Do I feel aligned with the organization and my team in terms of personal integrity?

Do I sense organizational integrity beyond the "mission statement"?

Can you really help this company? Is it an opportunity that "fits" you? Is it worth spending your life doing what the opportunity indicates you will be doing? OR, is this about a paycheck?

Is this what I really want? Will it benefit my family? Leverage my skills? Use my passion(s)? Am I genuinely excited about doing this?

Stop and really think about your answers to these questions as you look over the blues and reds on your YBR. *Listen to your intuition and what your internal discernment tells you*. Do you know? Stop and consider all the times in your life you have not paid attention to the feeling you have deep inside about something being offered to you. It turned out to be a mistake, burning months, years or even decades of time, right? If so, you need to honor your inner wisdom, and take time to really seek to identify what it is indicating to you about the opportunity at hand. People who are "desperate jobseekers," and those simply chasing a paycheck are *most susceptible* to this type of thinking and poor choices. They are EXCELLENT at NOT listening to their inner voice, and as a result, are often finding themselves living the life that contributes to them feeling miserable and feel like they are "missing their life purpose." Is this you? Stop and consider the following definition...

> **A Miserable Life = Living A Life You Don't Want, Working In a Job You Hate**

We can't emphasize enough the importance of knowing yourself, knowing what you are looking for, and trusting the process of finding a "good fit" opportunity. You should feel or sense inner peace as you make important decisions regarding the question: Is this a good fit? You will discover what you are looking for when you listen to, understand, and respect your personal needs, being honest about what works and *why.*

The X-Factor

In the process of determining if the opportunity is a "good fit," be aware of *unknowns* that we refer to as the "x-factor." X-factors are simply the unknowns that you respond to throughout the interview or opportunity interaction process. These x-factors shed light on how you truly feel about the person you are talking to. You will find that the longer or more frequent the interactions, the more "x-factors" come into focus. These x-factors are important across the opportunity spectrum, no matter if it is for a contract-based opportunity, a true full-time job, or an entrepreneurial gig. X-factors surface when you discover answers to the following important questions:

- **Like:** Do I really like these people?
- **Trust**: Do I trust these people? Why or why not?
- **Fit**: Do I fit in with these people? Do I want to associate with them? Hang out with them?

Think about times where you have really fit in well to a team, an organization, or an assignment. When you think about these times, people you like and trusted were involved. There was integrity embedded in the situation that you could *sense*. There was positive emotion that caused the situation to move forward in a *pleasing and affirming way,* that had nothing to do with the "stated mission statement." Answering *honestly* the questions that address x-factors is critical, because if you don't honestly answer these questions and ignore them, the results come back again and again to haunt you.

Donna's story....

Donna knew from the initial times she met and interacted with the boss of an organization that he wasn't a good communicator or leader. A quiet introverted person herself, she sensed he was temperamental and short fused, as often peers she talked to in the interview process walked (and also talked) on *eggshells* when he was present. Donna flat out "needed the paycheck" and sensed at her age she should just be happy for a j-o-b so she took the work, even though she had reservations about this boss.

Shortly, as she went to work for him, her intuitive feelings about worse case scenarios on this particular boss came to surface when in weekly tirades he would publicly belittle her work efforts and use her as an emotional punching bag. These horrific interactions would leave her feeling self-defeated, sad, and genuinely depressed. She would also greatly fear the next thing that would "set him off" and found herself increasingly anxious about details of her work that used to come easily to her.

She knew things had to change but lacked a process (and the support and required self-confidence) to move forward during a terrible employment situation. Through answering questions about the x-factor and admitting she did not listen to her intuition, she's defined what she wants, and equally *does not want* in her next opportunity or situation. While working to transition from the toxic situation she is in, she is simultaneously expanding her relational base, is working to refine the story of her, and is moving forward to explore opportunities that offer her an escape route from the "job from hell." Her accountability group is helping her to combat feelings of helplessness and inertia, reminding her not to settle again to simply move on from the toxic situation she's in. They are holding her accountable to make measurable progress toward her goals. They ask her probing questions that help her to recognize when her lack of confidence or self-worth impacts the way she presents herself considering new options.

 The story of you should be used like Cinderella's glass slipper. It should be tried on against every suitor and opportunity you are sincerely considering. Additionally, your human brand plays a very important role in the process. Just as you are asking if the situation is a "good fit," the people you are meeting with are asking the same question. Subtle things about you as a person play into their assessment of the x-factor associated with you. What types of things are they evaluating?

Energy: Do you have positive and vibrant energy? Or, do you seem to lack energy or enthusiasm? Are you a motivated person? What evidence do they have of your motivation, follow through, and ability to be proactive?

Sophistication: Are you up with or comfortable with latest technologies, trends, or developments in your industry? What do your social online posts indicate about your industry knowledge? Abilities?

Authenticity: Are you presenting a "façade" of what they want to hear, or are you being authentic to whom you are? Are you in any way being vulnerable? Is there "junk in your emotional trunk"?

Outlook: Are you an optimistic person or a pessimist? Do you affect or infect others?

Trustworthiness: Are you trustworthy? Does your story make sense? Can they sense your integrity as a person, as a professional?

Likableness: Are you likable? How would you fit into their team? Their culture? Their values?

Personal Presentation: While "dress for success" is a somewhat out dated notion, the bottom line is that *how* you present your physical presence as you meet others *absolutely matters* and leaves a solid impression, positive or negative. You need to reflect the culture and presentation style of those you are talking to. Are your clothes clean? Are they pressed and wrinkle free? Are your clothes current in terms of style? Is your hair clean and is the style or cut up to date? Does your hair betray your age, or does it help keep age a "non-issue"? How about the style and frame of your glasses? Your jewelry, does it make noise? Does it distract? How about your make-up? Are your nails tidy and clean? Do you look camera ready? What do your choices of color, style or presentation say about you? How about your breath? Are you chewing gum during an interview? If it's an outdoor lunch, are you keeping your sunglasses on when they want to look in your eyes to see how you respond to questions? Really, think about how you are presenting yourself. Here are a few examples of how minor things can make major impact.

Great glass frames on an otherwise completely unmemorable candidate: One guy who interviewed for a company wore beige pants, a white shirt and dark shoes to an interview with me. He was plain as a person and personally unmemorable as a candidate, except that he had very commanding and professional glass frames that added a "frame of credibility" to his otherwise ordinary face. His glasses were edgy and fashion forward. They were a singular "confident" choice against an otherwise almost completely beige blank canvass. It worked for him and gave him an air of authority and credibility that as a candidate he needed to stand out from others. *Yes, simple glass frames did this for him.*

Long, thinning hair on a 60+ woman: One exceptionally talented woman interviewed for multiple supply chain management leader opportunities. Her hair was as she had worn it since high school: processed blond, long, thinning, and on this day quite greasy. She had beautiful blue eyes, a sincere face and story, yet horrifically bad hair that was distracting from her otherwise pleasant personal persona. To say the long, outdated hair hurt her search efforts is an understatement. It immediately drew attention to the one thing she did not want to focus on, her age.

Stained clothes tell a bigger story on the call center candidate: One woman with a beautiful voice desired to work in a call center. Her challenge? Her personal presentation, ability to plan, and willingness to be held responsible. Her clothes told a story contributing to others impression of her. This otherwise talented person simply did not pay attention to how and when she ate. *She did not like keeping a schedule.* Her personal habits resulted in her often choosing to eat fast food in her car on her way to an interview or at a new job. She would inadvertently get chili cheese dog with onions on her blouse and pants, and/or (worse) carry the food with her into the work environment. Often, she was pressed for time because she did not factor in parking, so she would frequently be late to work or events she had said she'd be at. Long story short, she was often unclean, eating at her desk (which others did not appreciate), and did not care how her choices impacted the workspace of others. Her personal habits led to her being let go, repeatedly. In becoming knowledgeable of her personal habits, her clothes told a story that was not far behind her first impression. No matter how many companies tried to hire her and work with her situations, it took her accountability group confronting her on her behaviors, excuses, and attitudes to let her know that she shared in responsibility for the way employers (and other employees) felt about her at work.

You Have Control...

Over many things, including your human brand, the x-factor, your ability to leave a strong and clear impression with everyone you meet, your ability to move "opportunities in and out of the YBR pipeline." These are all things that you can control. Too often, if you have been in transition for an extended amount of time, or are preparing for transition, you might feel that there is little you can control. *This simply is not true.* There is much you can control, and a "good footprint" is one of the things you can intentionally do that can make a significant difference.

What Is a Good Footprint?

You should be reinforcing your value at *every* interaction. How do you accomplish this? Two ways. First, by presenting a solid "human brand," and second, by leaving a detailed paper trail that conveys the purpose of the conversation and the understandings established during the conversation.

A good footprint is just what it sounds like, a "footprint that stays with a company that leads them back (uniquely) to you." The goal of your "footprints" is that you make it easy for someone you meet with inside a company to communicate your value and status to others. If done well, your contact can forward your documentation on with little further detail as the "footprint" is somewhat self-explanatory. In follow up documents you might provide mini-case studies of your accomplishments, examples that further illustrate an idea, leadership strategy or philosophy, or detailed references to problems you've solved for other organizations that parallel the needs of the company you are speaking with. Examples and templates for each type of "good footprint" documents are provided in the tools section associated with this module. Read the examples before you draft your versions, as it will provide the level of detail that will help answer questions, clarifying your approach.

Examples of a Good Footprint:

Bio: A high level, short but detailed document that provides an overview of your skills, value and history to date. This is different from a resume. The only way we suggest you submit a resume is if it is customized (thus meaningful) to those reviewing it.

Thank-You Note: A well-written personal note of appreciation that demonstrates *personal and professional* attention to opportunity details. It conveys sincere appreciation or enthusiasm for the opportunity presented, and further enhances the essence of your human brand.

Value Proposition or Discussion Document: This is a customized document you create that *expands* upon key questions asked, or topics that were raised in a conversation. It may be sent as a follow-up document to a call or an in-person discussion. *This document summarizes specific details associated with your situational understandings, providing deliverables associated with direct and measurable value that you intend to add to the company (or opportunity) you are pursuing.* It paints the picture of *your unique talent* and experiences, equating these experiences or skills to specific issues that the company wants you to address in order for them to ascertain the value (deliverables) you will deliver in working with them. The document may address problems you will solve, efficiencies you will create, new forms of revenue you can deliver, strategic partners you can introduce that provide market advantage, leadership and direction or intellectual processes (IP) that will create new revenue, measurable advantage or market opportunity in association with your efforts. The point of this document is to identify specific deliverables you will deliver that add value to each person *or department* who is part of the decision-making process. These align with unique value and solutions that you *and only you* can provide (no one else can provide your experiences, they are yours!).

You are connecting your personal and *measurable value* to what the opportunity requires for you to demonstrate "right fit." For each departmental head you interview with (or person in the decision-making process) you will want to customize the document to their unique concerns. You want to validate that you have heard their specific concerns or questions and have considered a solution tailored to meet their needs. Keep in mind that what people will always remember is how you make them feel, which is why these details are required as an important reference. Your goal is to have them forward this document to others simply saying, "Read this and you will know why I like/endorse/want to hire this person." You must communicate your own value proposition because, IF you leave this task to others, they will not do it properly or as well as you can.

On-site Presentation: This could come earlier or later in the "in person" discussion process (associated with managing blues), but it is essential that if you are asked to provide a meaningful presentation for all those that attend, you do it well. You want to tailor content to the audience needs, discussing things in plenty of detail for the time (and team) provided, positioning squarely your value (measurable value) to them. In this instance you might be presenting several case studies on how you solved similar challenges that the company, department or division faces. Do a product demo, speak to how you've led similar teams or overcome similar strategic market challenges that resulted in revenue, new markets, channels, partners, opportunity, innovation, etc...

 Addendum: Much like a Discussion Document, an Addendum is a document that addresses a specific topic or question raised during discussion or as requested. An addendum might include portfolio examples, additional personal or professional references, specific research samples, summarized industry intelligence, or any number of things that might be requested or referred to during the course of dialog that you want to provide your decision maker(s).

Proposal for Services: If you are positioning as an entrepreneurial resource, contractor, consultant, or service provider, you will need to have a clearly written proposal for services. In this document you will outline a detailed scope of services to be provided, identifying the timeline for delivery, and stipulations impacting this timeline or proposed pricing for delivery. You will include your terms for payment, location to send payment (perhaps options for payment if you want to offer various types of terms or payment options), as well as federal employer ID. It is encouraged to also list out in detail any resources you require the client to provide in advance or during the project.

This is an important nuance: _Never_ describe a "proposal for services" as a "bid for services." Why is this? Even if it is common to use the word in the industry you serve, there are many reasons to never use the word "bid" instead of proposal for services. Reasons to ban the word "bid" from your vocabulary include:

Just the word "bid" indicates that you are "bidding" against something or someone! It infers that there is competition! Never bring on comparative competition to something you have worked hard to position as an exclusive "opportunity." This is an opportunity you have developed for yourself (and your unique qualifications). If you have done the process properly to this point, you have positioned exclusive value that you alone can deliver. This in mind, it is important not to compromise your position of strength by referring to your proposal as a "bid."

The word "bid" draws a focus to the issue of price (not value). You are competing on value, not price. The word "bid" almost immediately draws attention to a bottom-line number, which while relevant, should not be a definitive factor for decision making because the issue of price versus value should have been explored during the blue phase of determining "is this a fit?"

Finally, the word bid is frequently followed by the nasty little phrase "apple to apple comparison." My friend, you aren't an apple, so you don't want to be compared to others in this fashion. You offer a unique solution that only your experience qualifies you to deliver. While there may be some notion that other people like you exist "out there," in terms of the opportunity that you have uncovered and positioned for, they don't! There is one you. You need to propose your services, not bid against others in what can evolve further into a "line item comparison" of bids.

Detailed Voicemail: A detailed voicemail is clear, concise and cordial. It accomplishes in short order the purpose of the call and provides the listener with the option not to return the call if no response is required. Things to be aware of when leaving a voicemail:

- Making it clear who is calling (and if the listener might not remember you, how they know or met you)
- Making clear the point or purpose of the call
- Avoiding long, rambling recordings, or words such as "um" and "like"

The role of technical expert and closer in conveying the value and presentation of meaningful documentation is important. You are providing enough detail (assuming these mindsets) that you are moving the conversation forward in a very progressive and specific way. In the process of leaving a "good footprint" you are essentially creating a very structured argument for "why you." You are presenting critical information that conveys expertise, explains your uniqueness, and squarely positions the value that you can deliver (at the associated cost). In as many instances as possible, you are offering quantification of your proposed value so that you are presenting logic that relates to how clearly you are creating "return on investment."

What Is a Good Footprint Killer?

What is the best way to define a "good footprint" killer? The answer is to not do what you should or say you will do. These types of behaviors include:

No meaningful documentation: You get to the end of dialog (associated with qualifying a blue lead in your pipeline) and there is no clear "next step" or call back date for follow-up. At the end of each interaction, the "next step" should be clear, and a date with completing it selected. A footprint killer is when after an initial dialog, it is not clear what value you provide or *how* you will address specific requirements associated with the role, contract or opportunity you are pursuing. In providing no meaningful documentation or further communications, you are being passive in the process, and not showing initiative unless the person interacting with you specifically states that you are not to provide further information or details.

Sketchy details, poorly written communications, incomplete information or lack of follow-up: The quality of information you are providing is critical. Much like the attention that goes into re-reading and proof-reading a resume or bio, you need to be thorough in reviewing the quality of your work. If the information you are providing is confidential in nature, state that it is to be held in confidence. Providing examples or case studies, please make sure you are not disclosing sensitive information relating to a former employer or client.

Poorly presented human brand: Ask, do they like you, trust you? Think you will fit in? Keep in mind that your human brand encompasses your digital brand (social presence and footprint left via social media posts in addition to what you provide). Many potential business associates or employers will review your Facebook posts, LinkedIn profile, Twitter posts, Instagram accounts or other types of social platforms you may be posting on. It is important that you ask the following questions about your social media posts, or what a Google search would reveal about you personally and professionally:

-How would what I am posting culturally fit in at the company I'm interviewing with? Would they appreciate this humor? Political perspective? Religious viewpoint? Photo of me? Or random comment?

-Does this post make me seem moody? Depressed? Anxious? Sad? Unreliable? Overly sensitive? Easily offended? Gossipy? What does it reveal about my character? Integrity? Sense of values?

-Am I authentic in the transition from cyberspace to real world? Or, am I "one way" online and another way entirely in an interview?

-Does what you post on LinkedIn add to your professional credibility? How complete is your LinkedIn profile? Is your photo outdated, does it look professional or like a sports shot? Have you asked for written professional endorsements? How robust is your professional network? Looking at your profile, what deductions can be made about you professionally? Personally (are you active in the community, how are you personally giving back to others)?

-If you are a woman, it should be noted that research on professional dress suggests that *perceived power* is proportionate to coverage in dressing. A lot of skin showing equates to less perceived power. No matter what is in fashion when choosing attire, choose carefully. Choose to err on the side of being conservative, as it contributes to perception of power.

Myth: You Get Hired For Your "Talent"

There is a myth that permeates the workplace and mindset of those looking for opportunity. The myth (and associated mindset) is this: *It is all about talent, skills and performance.* Guess what? While these things are important, they are *not* the primary reason that people are hired, contracted or given opportunity. *In fact, these are secondary reasons people hire you.* The primary reason people hire you. They like you and trust you. This is a fact. Struggling to believe this? Stop and think about it. If a creepy AC guy walks into your home and you do not like or trust him (even if he has extraordinary technical skills) you won't hire him to fix the AC! This is a stunningly simple concept, yet people fail to factor it in and exploit it to their advantage when connecting with people to uncover opportunity. Recent research on MBA students interviewing for jobs suggested that candidates spent *so much time* in the initial interview trying to demonstrate their qualifications that they failed to *personally* connect with the person conducting the interviews! This lack of personal connection contributes to more "highly qualified" people being passed over then almost any other factor. And, it begins early in the process. Your chances of getting hired are 1 in 7 if someone refers you to an opportunity, opening the door with their relationship according to a study by MSNBC.

Transitioning to the Role of Closer

As you work through the process of meeting with decision maker(s) and leaving a good footprint, you are leading toward "closing the opportunity." What this means is that you will ask for a job, contract or opportunity to be awarded to you! To do this, you need to think like a "closer." Some people might feel odd in actually asking for the opportunity but stop and consider the impact you will have when you go through the entire relationship development process and defend your value. You are prepared to close the opportunity because good fit has been determined, and it is more about terms and conditions (which are addressed in the next module, "Module Eight: Negotiate Compensation And Close").

Let us recap from the beginning where you are at in the process of moving opportunities through your YBR. You generated a Yellow from contacting Whites (who are names of people you know or want to know) on your MAP. You found the Yellow opportunity by thinking and acting like a Prospector, Agent, Headhunter and Connector. Once the opportunity indicates they are ready to meet to discuss a funded (real) opportunity, job, contract or project, the Yellow is re-classified as a blue. You then meet with the Blue as a Technical Expert and Recruiter to slow down and determine if the opportunity is a "good fit." You are focused on quality of the fit, not quantities of the opportunities! You are carefully asking the eight questions to really understand the prospect's (or employer's) definition of success. You are positioning your unique value, getting clarification of critical details, and crafting a proposal or "good footprint" that outlines how you will use your best talent (and warehouse of skills) to address their needs and create measurable value.

Once a person at a Blue meeting asks for a proposal from you, the Blue opportunity on your YBR immediately reclassifies to a Red and you change hats one more time moving from the Technical Expert to the Closer. In the next module, we will discuss what this means as you prepare to negotiate and close the deal, reinforcing your value every step along the way.

Closing An Opportunity

At every blue interaction you are establishing further understandings, establishing your value, and positioning yourself to ask if this is a good fit or not. When it is a good fit, and you are asked for a proposal for your services (your job requirements, PO, contract RFP or "bid"), you need to think and act like a closer.

Here is an illustration of how to think and act like a closer...

Ruth was at her fourth company meeting when she was pulled in spontaneously to meet with the Partner of the tax firm she was interviewing with. Things were going very smoothly, and after extended conversation with him, he asked her what it would take for her to join the team. Where this is a perfect opportunity to indicate her salary range and level of interest in doing the work, and joining the team, she shyly asked for a range, and then mentioned she knew he was talking to a number of other candidates. Does this sound like a closer? No. *It sounds like someone still unsure of their value or uncertain of the fit.*

When she encountered clear indication that he is interested in her, her response ought to have been "Well Paul, I'm excited to hear this as I feel after visiting with your team that ACME is a solid cultural fit for me. I genuinely like the team and could see myself fitting in and adding measurable value. My range is $X-X depending on benefits. Will this work for you? If it's appropriate, I'd like to set a time with you to talk about my 30/60/90 day priorities for the position, so that in advance of a start date, I can prepare to onboard quickly and hit the ground running. Would this make sense to you? What date would work best for you? Should I meet with anyone else in advance of this meeting? I want you and the team to know I am available to you and look forward to working with HR to get the paperwork done...

Exercise 1: Update MAP And YBR

In your accountability group, or with your partner, discuss (approximately 10 minutes):

- Your progress filling out your MAP, choosing contacts and meeting with them to find potential opportunities
- Your progress filling out your YBR, listing opportunities you are tracking as Yellows, Blues, and Reds
- How are things going with your accountability partner? What is working well so far? What could be improved? Think time management, clarity of interpersonal feedback, clearer personal goals or timelines, perhaps more aggressive goals

Exercise 2: Identify And Take Action On "Good Footprint" Opportunities

Ask, who have you met with recently you need to follow up with? How could you create a "good footprint" in your follow up efforts with them? Have you reviewed notes over your conversation with them to recall the true hot button issues that they wanted to discuss in greater detail? How could documentation reinforce or further illustrate stories you shared, or data that is important to consider when weighing you as a candidate or potential service provider?

Further, do you feel you have created a clear value proposition, and that they understand how your best talent or warehouse of skills will meet their needs? If not, how can your documentation address this deficit?

Was there anyone in the decision-making process with whom you should follow up and provide more detailed information?

Exercise 3: Pivot On The Spot

Scenario: "Well, we're really only looking for a junior assistant. You seem to have a lot more experience."
- Your response?
- Answer:
- What might you say?

Scenario: "Can you tell me in as much detail as possible exactly how you would solve our problem?"
- Your response?
- Answer:
- What might you say?

Scenario: "We aren't sure you are a fit for the role. While you have a lot of experience, we are not sure it aligns with our needs. What makes you believe you are a fit?"
- Your response?
- Answer?
- What might you say?

Scenario: You are approaching the end of the interview and want to know where you stand.
- Your response?
- Answer:
- What might you say?

Exercise 4: Review And Improve Key Documents

By now, you know that every document needs to be customized in order to be meaningful to the reader. You also recognize that each document serves an important function in reinforcing the value of your human brand. It's important to ask those you trust (such as your accountability partner) to review your bio, resume, LinkedIn profile, addendum examples, or proposal with a fresh eye to make sure these aren't dated, incomplete or "generic." In the spirit that almost anything can be improved, take a good look at every item you have in circulation, and make sure that it is as professionally done as possible.

While in the discovery process, you need to craft "good footprint" communications to illustrate your value to everyone you meet. The following examples demonstrate different types of approaches you might use.

The goal is to craft a document that is detailed and clear, aligning your value with the concerns of the person reviewing the letter. By making this effort you are demonstrating that you have heard them. You are presenting detail about experiences that relate to their challenges describing how you would add value and address their challenges.

The purpose of the document is to make it very simple for the reader to forward it onto others who they want to "get up to speed" in terms of their opinion of you as a candidate or solution provider.

Example One:

January 17, 20XX
MS. TAMMY JENSEN PRESIDENT AGRICAREERS, INC.
HWYS 148 AND 92
WEST MASSENA, IA 50853

RE: BUSINESS UNIT MANAGER POSITION

Dear Tammy,

Thank you for taking time to visit with me this afternoon. I thoroughly enjoyed our conversation, as well as the insights you were able to provide, with respect to the Business Unit Manager position. From our conversation and through my research, several issues surface as being key to the success of not only the new Business Unit Manager, but also to the company as a whole. As an addendum to my resume, I would like to take this opportunity to address these issues, both to ensure my understanding of the key challenges of the position, and to also offer suggestions and/or examples of how I might address them as the Business Unit Manager. Furthermore, the following is subject to change as I receive additional details:

1. Team Spirit, Inclusion, A feeling of Belonging, A "Big Picture" point of view, Esprit de Corps.
As organizations grow, individual business units, satellite plants, etc., naturally move further away from the parent. I have experienced this in several companies, to varying degrees. In such cases, I have found that "Leadership," as opposed to "Management" is a key to bringing people together.

Additionally, I have been successful taking key rank and file team members with me on corporate trips, including them in corporate training sessions, and even taking them on customer visits.

Upon their return to the plant, they simply can't stop talking about all they have seen and have done, making the others feel as though they were there as well. In addition to these trips, I also like to include corporate news and highlights in my monthly "all hands" update meetings. This is accomplished by using PowerPoint slides and photographs. It is also effective to solicit my boss and other key leaders to address the group whenever time and schedules allow. In combination, these individual activities are powerful tools that can be used to build a strong and cohesive team.

Finally, one must remember that it is not only important to bring corporate issues to the business unit, but that it is also important to take business unit issues and accomplishments to the corporation. A feeling of trust and mutual respect must be obtained and maintained, which facilitates a free flow of information in both directions. It is through both these actions and communications that real teamwork is realized.

2. Increase sales, increase market share, and improve the success of new product introductions.

As the General Manager of CTB's Poultry Production Systems Business Unit, I was successful in leading an increase in sales from $21.3M to $31.9M, an increase of nearly 50%, from July 2001 to July 2004. During this same time, Operating Income increased from $2.9M to $9.4M. How did this happen?

Several things took place over this period. In brief:
1. I replaced my National Sales Manager, with an internal candidate.
2. I combined Sales and Marketing into one position.
3. Some number of price increases were implemented.
4. Four major new products were introduced into the market.
5. Through acquisition, a product line was added to our offering.
6. I, as well as the rest of the staff, became a part of the sales force.

With the assistance of my new National Sales Manager, goals and objectives were established, as were incentives for achieving and exceeding these goals. We let the District Sales Managers know that this was a new day and that we/they needed to perform better.

Though I had worked with Sales departments for many years in the past and had 10 years of experience on the other side of the desk, as a Buyer, I needed to learn more about sales.

To this end, my National Sales Manager and I spent countless hours role playing, going over strategies, reviewing market data, learning the different features of each product, etc., until we both felt comfortable with the direction we were headed.

To become more familiar with him and his management style, he and I took several road trips, both to visit various District Sales Managers, as well as customers. Again, the plan became more solid.

To learn, firsthand, how our products solved the problems of the end users, I rode with each of the District Sales Managers, one week per year, listening to them and to our customers. On a couple occasions, I was also able to participate in the installation of the equipment, at the farm. These activities strengthened my relationships with not only the salespeople, but also with our customers. They began to trust and understand me, but more importantly, I knew that I could trust them, and now I knew at least some of their challenges.

To learn even more of their issues, a "Listening Tour" was established, during which time end users and distributors gathered together with my respective salespeople and me, solely for the purpose of hearing what they had to say, listening to their issues and challenges, listening to their suggestions, and answering their questions as best we could. Through these sessions and the other activities, we were able to not only introduce major new products, but also many modifications of existing products, all of which contributed to our success.

3. Operational improvements, process improvements and increased efficiency and productivity.

As a rule, happy people are productive people. Furthermore, their attendance is better, their quality is better, and they accept ownership of that to which they have been entrusted. I have grown businesses, improved communications, and resolved multiple conflicts through the consistent and fair management of staff at all levels. I am highly skilled at bringing a diversity of people and cultures together to pursue a common goal, at improving health, safety, and workplace life, both inside my facility and of those of my suppliers and customers. This I have accomplished through organizational re-structuring, fair and objective appraisal systems, hands on leadership, genuine care for people and effective communications. I routinely conduct monthly plant wide informational/project update meetings, and form cross-functional teams to address challenges and issues.

While involved in a project, I endeavor to identify both internal and external process steps, establishing bite-sized but firm goals and objectives, hold bi-weekly update meetings for the purpose of celebrating wins and resolving misses. Then, upon completion of the project, I conduct team presentations to management, followed by a victory thank you and a celebration.

With any role, it is imperative that the people involved not only have the right set of tools, but also understand which tool to use and how to use it. One such set of tools is referred to as Lean Enterprise.

I have been a Lean practitioner for nearly my entire career, sometimes under a different name, both as a student and as a teacher. Lean Enterprise, process improvement, and/or continuous improvement are invaluable, when used to improve processes, reduce waste, increase throughput rates, increase productivity and decrease scrap and downtime. Additionally, I am Six Sigma Green Belt Certified, which aids in further quality improvements and long-term solutions to challenges.

There are no magic pills. It all requires a lot of work and dedication. I like to begin my day by walking through the manufacturing plant, seeing firsthand where we are, learning what the issues are and how they are being addressed. I like to talk with the operators on the floor, as they are more than willing to let you know how it "really is." I want them to see that I know what is going on and that I care both about them and about the company. I want them to tell me about their families, and I want them to see my anguish as I make difficult policy decisions. Through it all a bond is formed, and a team is created, one that will unite to resolve all of the issues at hand and increase returns.

It is my most sincere desire to utilize my knowledge, experience and talents to increase the sales and profitability of the company I am associated with, to improve the overall work environment, and to position the organization for future growth, while enriching not only the lives of the owners or stockholders, but also those of the entire staff. My success in this endeavor will then enable me to give back more to the community and to the multitudes in need of care and attention.

Again, I am extremely interested in joining a company where my management style and personality is compatible with the other members of the executive staff, and where I can put my knowledge and experience to work increasing the overall value of the company and to assisting those around me to achieve their highest potential.

Thank you for your time and consideration, and I look forward to taking the next steps.

Respectfully,

Donald C. Mueller

Example 2:

January 17, 20XX
Mr. Clay Graham AGCO
420 West Lincoln Blvd.
Hesston, KS 67062

Clay:

Thank you for taking time to meet with me on Tuesday. It was helpful to learn more about AGCO and the Operations Manager position open at the Hesston facility. I would also like to commend your staff on their professional and courteous treatment prior to, and during my visit. Regina, Darin, and Chris were all extremely helpful during the process.

Per our conversation about the company and the position, I have outlined below high-level thoughts on how I could provide value to your organization:

- Communicate the case for change and champion the transformation to a culture of continuous improvement.
  Example: I have over 10 years of successful experience introducing, implementing, and sustaining lean initiatives in several locations within Goodyear. Implementation of pull systems (kanbans) in our Topeka plant has reduced WIP by more than 33% while at the same time reducing the waste of waiting for product. I have facilitated kaizen events resulting in significant material waste reductions, improved changeover times, and safety improvements. I also have a proven ability to engage the floor and enlist their participation in being part of the solution during these activities. More importantly, I have been successful in implementing systems that allow us to sustain and improve upon the gains that we have realized because of kaizen events.
- Talent Development.
  Example: In my current and past assignments, I have facilitated leadership development classes focused on providing tools essential to first-line managers' success on the factory floor. Those classes were proven successful by the improved performance of the managers participating in those sessions.

Clay, you mentioned some concern about the job level. I would like to reiterate to you that my focus is on the job *fit* ... how I would fit within and contribute to the success of the team. Based on what I learned Wednesday, I am confident that my skills and abilities are in alignment with the needs of your organization to meet the challenges and objectives of the company.

Thank you again for your time and I look forward to receiving an offer.

Regards,

Mike Burns

Example 3:

January 18, 20XX

Mr. George Brown
Managing Director
Villa Chateau Estate
In care of Ms. Mary Stone

Dear Mr. Brown:

Please consider the following addendum to my resume to provide further insight towards my capabilities and approach toward building Villa Chateau in the United States market. From conversations with Mary Stone and through research, several issues surface as being keys to the success of not only the new Country Manager position, but to the brand and company. I would like to address these issues, both to ensure my understanding of the key challenges of the position and offer suggestions and/or examples of how I might address them as the Country Manager.

Situation Analysis

If appointed, I would immediately undertake both quantitative and qualitative analysis of the current situation. These measures will be monitored and reported against on a regular basis to ensure ongoing success. This would allow deep understanding of the current state of Villa Chateau in the United States. Key analytics to include:

1. Depletion Tracking – a critical measure of distributor/importer performance.
2. State-by-State Benchmarking – understand volumes as related to market potential/size.
3. AC Nielsen Trend Analysis – how the brand responding versus market/peers in the retail environment.
4. Financial Analysis – understanding internal profitability and resources available for the brand.
5. Distributor Interviews – based on my relationships at senior levels of all major distributors, understand the issues and opportunities facing the brand from the wholesaler's perspective.
6. Customer Feedback – engage priority customers on their history and opinions toward the brand.
7. Import Agreement – need understanding of legal expectations and obligations.
8. Price and Positioning – exploration of price strategy versus marketplace.

Execution Management

Every salesforce needs clarity towards expectations and resources. Like my previous roles, I would immediately establish clear sales objectives towards sold accounts (both on/off-premises), SKU level depletions and shipment budgets, and financial contribution.

This shall need to be accomplished through collaboration with Vineyard Brands to ensure sufficient "buy-in." Based on preliminary analysis, there are some apparent execution issues challenging Villa Maria:

1. Depth and Quality of Distribution – as evident by low ACV and declining sales trends.
2. Product Mix and Prioritization – as evident by Sauvignon Blanc being 89% of brand sales mix (per AC Nielsen).
3. Key Customer Voids – limited National Account coverage.

4. On-Premises Prioritization – high profile by-the-glass exposure is necessary.

Due to my depth of both distributor and key customer (National Account) management experience, I am uniquely positioned to "gap-fill" any situations where Vineyard Brands is either under-resourced or lacks the relationship/capability to successfully drive execution. This is a delicate balance requiring both situational and self-awareness to deftly manage the importer relationship. Self-awareness is a strength that will serve me well in working effectively on behalf of the brand while not eroding the necessary relationship with Vineyard Brands along the way. I would plan to approach the current importer respectfully and collaboratively, all while challenging them to improve execution immediately. My experience as an importer, supplier, and distributor equips me with the necessary tools to build a quality relationship with the current importer.

Refine Brand Profile and Consumer Message
The main challenge with every brand is clarity of identity. What does Villa Chateau want to be, and how is this communicated internally with trade partners, and externally with consumers? As this question is answered, I normally take a strategic approach as both "steward" and "shaper" of this message. Throughout my career with specific experience towards imports, brands have had mixed success in resonating with the American consumer. The brands that succeeded tailored a consistent and clear (global) brand message and adapted it to fit the American consumer.

The brands that struggled simply relied upon a global marketing strategy, and "one-fits-all" approach. With such learning in mind, I shall immediately seek to understand the core elements of the Villa Chateau brand proposition and propose both supplements/additions to global initiatives, while forwarding suggestions for both new messages and modes of "awareness-building" communication. Key areas of focus should include:
*   Public Relations – strategic sampling, media outreach, and event participation.
*   Website – usefulness and content to match trade partners and consumer needs.
*   Trade Marketing – customer-centered marketing programs in support of strategic feature activity.
*   On-line Partnering – search engine optimization, direct-to-consumer options, viral/buzz marketing.

Create Ideal Route to Market Strategy and Structure
Villa Chateau, as evident through the creation of this position, seeks to improve their sales capability. This can be accomplished through either a third party or a dedicated sales footprint. As evident by the current brand position when evaluated against category competition, the results being driven by Vineyard Brands are insufficient. If appointed, I would provide an analysis of options and forward an ideal organizational development plan once ownerships desire and vision towards volume, profit, supply, and both short-term/long-term goals are understood.

In three different situations, I have either created or reshaped organizations based on the needs of the brands, marketplace fit, and economic condition. Please note a summary of each:
1. Northcorp Wines Ltd. My graduate school requirement for the sponsoring company was work on a critical issue facing the firm. I created a re-organizational proposal entitled "Match to Channel Re-organization Plan" to Southcorp leadership that was implemented across the firm.

2. Club Nathan USA Inc. acquired Trio Wines Inc. in June 2008. Refined the previous organization considering the new portfolio and marketplace requirements.

- Transformed an organization from volume-driven to profit-driven in a matter of six months.
- Created new roles and sales structure supporting a more fine-wine oriented portfolio.
- Shaped ideal distributor network through termination and appointment.
- Improved organizational capability in underdeveloped channels (on-premises and national accounts).
  Alignment of people, promotional support, and marketing budgets to priority trade channels.
- Improved customer intimacy with key trade partners.

3. Blue Wines Inc. In September 2005, I founded an innovative import company based on the Australian category voids at the time. Widely regarded as best in class by the distributor network, Cumulus drove amazing results very quickly. Some key outcomes:

- Created a nationwide import business within three months (entity creation, compensation plan, development, employees hired, customers pre-sold and national distributor network appointed).
  Eight of top ten national accounts sold within twelve months.
- Generated volumes of over 70,000 cases in 2006, and 100,000 cases in 2007.

I will craft the best Route-to-Market strategy based upon the brand owners' objectives, brand development strategy, and marketplace necessity. My historic relationships with all major distributors and resellers will prove to be an invaluable asset during this process. We will build the ideal platform to fuel Villa Chateau's ascent as an icon brand within the minds and mouths of the American consumer.

There are certain qualities or guiding principles to which I ascribe. Brand owners, distributors, customers, and employees alike value the absolute integrity by which I operate. Relationships are precious to me, and I place the highest degree of value on honest/transparent communication with business partners.

Thank you for your consideration. I look forward to meeting you to discuss this opportunity further.

Respectfully,

Ron Mertz

Example 4:

January 18, 20XX

Mr. Jim Keeney, Chief Financial Officer
KC Free Health Clinic
3515 Broadway
Kansas City, MO 64111

Dear Mr. Keeney:

It was a pleasure meeting with you Friday and I look forward to becoming further acquainted. Thank you so much for the opportunity to learn more about you and the KC Free Health Clinic.

After reflecting on our discussion regarding the Director of Human Resources opportunity, the following are *high-level* thoughts on how I might provide value to The Clinic:

Executive Summary
An integrity-driven and accomplished leader with 20 + years of Human Resources Generalist experience, who has an extremely strong customer service orientation, professional, loyal, adaptive, and dependable. I possess a strong mid-western work ethic, self-motivated, a superior listener and able to work effectively with all levels of the organization.

- **Advocate for the employees while balancing the needs of the organization.**
  Example: As the GAFRI office was nearing the shutdown I personally sent 400 letters to CEOs and HR Executives of area service organizations informing them that we had many good people looking for other opportunities. As I learned of open positions, I posted them, emailed the employees, and opened the office to these companies for job fairs. This resulted in many employees already having other opportunities to pursue upon their termination.

- **Assess the needs of individual contributors and the management team, identifying and implementing changes and development opportunities where warranted.**
  Example: Designed and implemented training in the areas of Ethics, Employment Law, Sexual Harassment, Coaching and Counseling, and Progressive Discipline. Considered a mentor and advisor to all.

- **Recruitment and retention of high-quality individuals.**
  Example: The average tenure of the population at GAFRI was 16 years and 65% of employees were in their current positions because of promotion from within. I measured the effectiveness of the recruiting function – turnover, including reasons for turnover and the quality of new hires. I trained managers on the legal aspects of interviewing and how to use behavioral interviewing by crafting interview questions to assess the knowledge, skills, and abilities of the candidate.

I am sincerely excited about the Director of Human Resources position and look forward to additional discussions. It would be a privilege to be part of your organization. I am confident in my ability to "hit the ground running" and contribute to the goals, objectives, and mission of the KC Free Health Clinic.

Your time and consideration are appreciated. Please feel free to contact me with additional questions.

Respectfully,

Jan Mathieu

Example 5:

September 10, 20XX

Mr. John Doe
Chief Executive Officer
ABC Company
12765 Opportunity Street, Suite 101
Bigtown, KS 66223

Dear Mr. Doe:

Good morning. I trust your day is going well. I thoroughly enjoyed our time together last week. I appreciated you sharing your entrepreneurial successes, and especially enjoyed hearing about your family.

As promised, I am getting back to you with some thoughts — and intended to do so sooner. My wife, Marie, and I had to head to Wichita last weekend to help our son relocate, and I am just now catching up. Who knew that a 23-year old grad student could have accumulated so much stuff!

Here are three observations I hope you will find of value:

1. It is apparent to me you follow a "servant leader" model and strive to empower your employees to achieve excellence. You care deeply, not only about your company, but also about your customers and employees. This was evidenced by the discussion about developing your technology person into the business manager and is indicative of your desire to improve your employees with a willingness to give them new opportunities. I would say that what you represent as a person, along with the type of leadership style you embrace, are huge positives, which many never develop. Your success is indicative of that. I would encourage you not to change. Something I have seen many times in the military is that there is often a fine line between taking care of your people and accomplishing the mission. If you will forgive me for being so direct, it sounds like there may be some team members who either don't share the same values — or maybe they just aren't clear on what the company (your) values are. That last part may well be the case, because "try as we might," we all sometimes have a hard time effectively sharing those with others in such a way that they really absorb the message about those things we are most passionate. I would encourage you not to change your style, but rather focus on building and developing your team to complement — not mirror — you and be multipliers for your strengths.

2. Your team is not where you want it right now. You want passionate hungry employees with a burning desire to be self-motivated to achieve excellence and your vision. You have talented individuals but at times it feels like they don't have the same commitment you have. I got the sense from our discussion that some have fallen into a rut or adopted a job "title" mentality and can't

move beyond that. They don't realize the tremendous opportunities that you are providing, or what awaits them through the company's success. The challenge is how do you motivate/evolve them from the "collecting a paycheck" mindset into a "value creation" mindset, which ultimately benefits all. In my experiences teaching empowerment is not an easy task. Those who have never experienced empowerment can't just do it and too often confuse empowerment with "not micro-managing." The beauty is once the true meaning of empowerment clicks in their head they become personally invested; this is a good place to be.

3. The military is known for its systems and/or processes as well as accountability. This is to ensure that during stressful times tasks are accomplished to standards without much "thinking."

You had mentioned a few things that caught my ear. You indicated that occasionally trucks leave without the needed equipment, which maintenance is an issue with an older fleet, and the cost of improperly placed signs is expensive and preventable. Preventive maintenance and services procedures as well as post mission After Action Reports (AAR) could mitigate some of your challenges. You mentioned you had procedures, but they were not always followed. Conducting standard daily opening and closing operations meetings could provide the checks and balances as well as help establish common understanding for the entire team.

Understanding it is easy to "armchair quarterback," please know my intent is to be helpful.

Thank you so much for the tour, lunch, pool but most importantly the conversation. I look forward to getting together again when your schedule permits.

Respectfully,

Jim Johnston

Recent Graduates Contributions Toward Company Profit

How do you actively prepare for the interview process? You need to be prepared to illustrate in interviews examples where you have assumed <u>responsibility.</u> This can be where have you lead in student activities, extra-curricular groups, held responsibilities associated with your hobbies or interest groups, in athletics or in non-profit activities.

How do you assume responsibility? You need to be able to discuss examples where you have done the following:

1. **Show Ownership**. You will need to be able to speak to and discuss examples of where you have "taken ownership" (showing you have ability to take the "good and bad" of any learning experience). So, where have you taken full responsibility for something? Example: Eagle Scout project, leading a club benefit event or fundraiser. Show humility to interviewer in discussing how you learned from elements of failure and success. Be able to provide examples of what you learned and how it has helped form your expectations of yourself moving forward.

2. **Set Standards**. Establishing standards and expectations in ways that anyone on your team can follow and understand exactly what needs to be done.
3. **Lead**. Assumed or volunteered leadership, or a support a "leadership" position.
4. **Create Measurable Value**. Offer innovation, efficiencies or new ideas for process improvement that result in measurable value to the organization or group you were working with.

The process of interviewing and starting your first "real opportunity"…

Keep in mind that your negotiation of value begins with your first handshake and personal impression with those you are meeting with. You want to be on time, dressed well (appropriate for the role and culture of the company you represent) and prepared in terms of having done research on the company or industry you are interested in.

Your goal in interviews and meeting with people is to understand from each person the scope of the work that needs to be done and how it needs to be done profitably. If you are meeting with people from multiple departments, keep in mind that you are tailoring questions to relate to the particular department.

When a company interviews you or hires you, what are their expectations? What should yours be? The following is a framework of understandings that should guide your focus on priorities associated with the work that needs to be done.

1. **Job one is to do your basic job. To do this you must understand the work that needs to be done.** What exactly are you hired to do? For example, in any business environment there are systems, terminology, processes. Your #1 priority is to get measurably proficient at the work you were hired to do. This is accomplished on several levels and is the foundation of your work. You must do your job and do it well, understanding it. Too often, new hires get distracted with other things.
   a. A typical assignment for a new hire? Do whatever the person who hires you tells you to do. We want you to understand that the value you add has to do with what and where you can add value by "taking ownership" of the process you have been asked to do. What do we mean by this? You become the expert by setting the standard and constantly IMPROVING the efficiency and effectiveness of what you are doing. Think in terms of standardization. CODE is a method for standardizing a process and can be a great way in which to break down a process. How are you consistently Communicating, Organizing, Documenting, or Evaluating every step of your work? To the degree you have templates, files and defined process, you can then focus on efficiency.
   b. Regarding tasks: Understand what you need to do. Document, take notes, pay attention to smallest details, ask questions (where do I find that file? Is there a template for this email?).

    c.   Do your work at a basic level of proficiency. Hopefully, the measures for productivity should be clear to you at hire. If it's a new role to the company, you might be helping your boss establish productivity expectations. These guidelines set expectations to describe how much work should be done per week or per day, or the way in which the value of your work is established.

    d.   Get really good at the work and seek to build expertise.

    e.   Eventually document and train others, even make improvements to the process or system.

- **Leadership:** It doesn't mean you are the boss. It's situational. When you see a small opportunity to take the lead, or take responsibility on a project, do it. Take something off your manager's or team's plate. Like what? Lead a meeting, prepare for the meeting (do pre-work in advance of the meeting), publish the notes or "to do list" at the end. Proactively identify areas where you can "take things on." Most teams have "daily meetings" amongst equals. More experienced people take on responsibility to take on development of the less experienced on the team, so the more experienced might be doing actual reporting on progress.

    a.   If someone lives in host city for a meeting, they may schedule rooms to meet in with a corporate host and set the agenda or plan activities for what team does when on site.

    b.   Other people put together teamwork plans. These plans identify who does what. They require an organized work schedule, work projections, budgets and expense management. Where can you contribute?

    c.   In business there are varying degrees of systems developed within the company you might work for. Typically, with truly small business, they may not have many formalized systems. It's the way Suzie "does it" over time. You need to help formalize systems and take ownership of processes because you may see more efficient or effective ways to do things using technology apps.

    d.   Leadership is about responsibility and committing to "take ownership" of things. Mature leaders then advise on strategies. They can advise on how to organize for work that's coming, how to prepare people and prep systems to expand. You need to recognize your need to prove yourself in small ways to others that lead you. Management can tell you constantly to "be strategic" about things, but until you have mastered how things are currently done (the work that needs to be done), how can you possibly advise about how things should be done?

    e.   You need to prove ownership of small things and do not be afraid of taking on the most small or "insignificant" jobs at a company because this is where you can prove your value. Keep in mind that excellent leaders are also typically people who are willing to serve in whatever way is required or is best for the team. Nothing is beneath them. When you act with a humble nature, it's so unusual in today's world that it almost immediately makes you stand out. Always know that anything you do in service to others exposes you to details that enhance your perspective of what needs to be accomplished. Improvement of process = efficiency and profit.

   f. Also, in this process you <u>gain trust</u> of others. This leads to additional responsibility and opportunity for growth.

2. **Take on additional responsibilities that add value to your team and boss.** Look for special projects outside the scope of "basic job" so you can increase expertise and value, skill development.

   a. There are often things that need to be done that no one wants to do, or nobody has volunteered for, that help your boss or colleagues/team. Perhaps someone needs to own administration of timesheets, or someone must administer permissions to software systems (setting up the users, privileges of users, and how is every new person and system added). This takes time and typically companies need at least one person to do this, who may be reluctant to take it on because it is tedious work.

   b. There may be things that you see that just should be done. These are situations where you proactively identify improvement, process or "something innovative or better" that needs to be put in place and you have the ability to do it.

   c. Attitudes: Come at it from a very respectful way. Things you might encounter:

     i. We've always done it this way and there's good reasons why.

     ii. In those situations, it's important for you to understand the WHY. Look for ways to incrementally improve the ways they've done it –respecting the history of why it's been done this way.

     iii. Until you understand the "why" of the way the system has been designed the way it has (systems have checks and balances), you can't really offer constructive criticism.

     iv. Respectful ways to interact with others. Demonstrate detailed knowledge. Take on small things, build trust and demonstrate respect to leadership by deferring to decisions that they make without grumbling or complaining to peers. This can be a difficult shift of attitude or behaviors because social media teaches us that our perspective or voice is always welcome. In work situations, this is simply not true. There's a time for feedback and you need to recognize when it is welcome with your boss or peers and when it is not.

- **Know your place and give things time.** You are going from a student to an employee. This is no easy transition. Why?

   a. Rules that have made you successful as a student *dramatically* change in the workplace. It isn't about you! In school it is all about you, what you want to do, how you do on tests, how you compete with others. As you transition from a school environment to the work world, the *exact opposite* is true. It's about others, how well you work to support your team and enable others via your management of responsibility and assumption of leadership moving forward.

   b. As a student you have autonomy. As a worker you have a lot less autonomy, particularly with technology and phone usage. At school, you can use it when you want. At work, it is inappropriate to use at times.

     i. Often, we've had executives who complain of catching quiet subordinates shopping or texting at a meeting by just glancing at their screen. This behavior comes across as inappropriate and *disrespectful*. Phone use while in meetings or in conversations can appear to be distracted and appear you simply aren't paying attention. A safe rule is no shopping, social media or planning a weekend.

ii.   On the other hand, if you are using technology to accelerate your learning, this is a different issue entirely. There are people who are searching "live" discussion topics or issues while in a meeting – and *if you ask upfront if this is okay* that you contribute live via your phone while in conversation with others – cool. Technology is a tool you can use to help benefit the company. The more likely you use technology in positive way, the more likely you will be to "get grace" when you do take a personal email or text. Just do not push it.

iii.   Distractions: Managing things that distract while working is critical. You need to be able to turn off alerts, your phone and stop engaging in habits that are not your primary job. Typically, if you are a new hire, you may get a warning about such infractions, but don't count on it. Be wise and just put away anything that might be a distraction (including texts).

3.   Got great ideas for the boss? Good, but be careful how you make suggestions. There is a CAREFUL balance of respecting the heritage of why a company has historically done things the way they have versus bringing new ideas and innovation to the table. How do you navigate new ideas that you might have?

   a.   Know the "why"- Why is this process done this way? Really understand how the system(s) that are in place have evolved over time and with technology application.

   b.   Ask, "how do I make my boss look good?" How do you make your team look good? How do I make my organization look good?

   c.   This is a team approach, not a competition. You are competing with business competition outside the office, not your colleagues. Share with them information or insights you have and enable them to do their work better.

   d.   You need to be able to build on what other people have done and be respectful of the traditions and culture of your workplace.

   e.   Culture is an extension of the people, a mini department within a larger department. Realize that every company has a personality and specific traits associated with the internal politics that impact the leadership associated with each department. From one department to the next, these traits may dramatically shift depending on the leadership personality of the department or company.

4.   It's not about you as an individual, but how you help everyone on your team and in your organization be more successful.

   a.   Share what you know, no hoarding of information. Even where you feel people aren't sharing with you, you need to proactively share with them. You can be in situations where you haven't been given access to information until you accomplish certain things, so don't make assumptions of why a colleague may have permissions or insights on things that you don't.

b. The more you <u>share information and skills with others,</u> the more valuable you become. This is not intuitive. As a student, you are expected to compete at tests against your peers. In the work world – just the opposite is true. You are expected to work as a team to help your company compete in the marketplace.

c. In school if you copy someone else's work, it is cheating. In the work world, asking others to utilize their ideas or existing processes is just smart. Being teachable, flexible, trustworthy, and adaptable is more important than being innovative. When you start work, you typically will do so on a team or in a department with lots of experienced co-workers to learn from.

5. Document your contributions and ask at the initial interview about measures that determine their definition of your success.

a. What is the company's definition for success in the role that you are interviewing for?

b. Should you be hired, what are the key performance indicators (KPI's) that the employer expects to see fulfilled?

c. If they don't have KPI's (and many small businesses don't yet have these defined), how will your work be measured in terms of value it delivers to the organization? If they do a 30, 60 or 90-day job review, what measures do you need to meet to meet or exceed their expectations? How will these measures be expected to change in 6 months? A year?

d. What does a career path look like within the company? What virtues do they value in relation to promotion to leadership? How do they tend to reward loyalty?

e. If you are offered an opportunity, understand that the "negotiation" for compensation starts at the first handshake. Once you understand how the company will measure the value of your work, then it's up to you to essentially convince the interviewer (if it's a good fit) that you've created essentially the same type of value before in assuming similar responsibilities, just not in the same role as this might be your first "real opportunity." This is accomplished by writing "thank you notes on steroids" that have addendums which are essentially mini-case studies of how you have created similar value for others in work or situations you have been associated with.

Accountability Meeting Agenda

0-15 *Review*

☐ Major events, how are you doing? How are you feeling about your progress? What you are learning?

☐ In the exercise on "pivoting," what made you stumble? How can you incorporate and practice this exercise of pivoting as an accountability group or in one on one practice efforts? Provide the group examples of "difficult pivots" you've had to do, explain how you approached the subject in question and felt that you performed a successful pivot.

☐ Homework: How does your documentation look? Can it be improved? How? What are your top priorities? Have your accountability partners reviewed your key documents to see if they can spot areas for improvement or customization?

15-30 Discuss

- ☐ Your MAP
- ☐ Your YBR
- ☐ Your next steps for opportunities identified, identify a specific list of "good footprint" strategies you can incorporate into your efforts

30-45 Temperature Check

- ☐ What's your attitude about what you are learning, how is your attitude(s) changing over time and exposure to the process?
- ☐ What behaviors are surfacing that surprise you?
- ☐ Are you meeting your goals? *If not, why*? How can these goals be adjusted to be "doable"?
- ☐ What skills need to improve? What is your plan to ask for help or evaluate potential resources?
- ☐ What key breakthroughs have you experienced? What have you learned about yourself? About others?
- ☐ How can you be encouraging and supportive of others?

45-55 Scoring and Closing Encouragement

- ☐ What one thing, if you could do it better, could really make a difference for you in terms of outcomes? What small step could you work into your efforts every day to make progress on this front?
- ☐ End with encouragement (what you admire or appreciate about your accountability partners)

Assignments for Next Session

- ☐ Read Module Eight: Negotiate Compensation
- ☐ Meet with your accountability partner(s)
- ☐ Continue to update and monitor your MAP and YBR progress daily
- ☐ Aim to contact five Whites opportunities this week
- ☐ Be aware of how you are investing your time this week. What are the biggest drains on your time or productivity? How can you slow down or stop these drains? Illustrations: One person we knew of that was struggling with watching endless hours on the new TV she bought unplugged it so that it was a hassle to turn on. She felt this extra step would provide her the self-reflection time to mindfully reduce her tendency to watch TV. It worked for her. Another person taped a handwritten check for the hourly rate of her consultative services to her computer so that when tempted to mindlessly web-surf, she was reminded of the true value of her time. This too worked. What steps can you take to address areas that are "time and energy wasters"? Brainstorm solutions for your partner and commit to at least trying the suggestions to see if you can't make small steps toward progress this week.

Module Eight: Negotiate Compensation And Close

Objectives

By the end of this unit, you will:

- Recognize how you might feel about the process of "negotiating compensation." You will become aware of how you internalize feelings that may impact your performance during this process
- Confirm that details associated with the work you have identified as an "opportunity" align with what you are truly passionate about
- Convey your value with confidence. You will realize that no matter with whom you talk or ultimately work with, you can deliver value (the only question is for whom and doing what)
- Use an ongoing discovery process to position and align your value from the first handshake
- Convey exactly how you can deliver measurable value to the company by connecting it to compensation that you feel is a fair return on your efforts
- Use "ballpark" dollar ranges to determine if the conversation of compensation is even appropriate
- Recognize that value is relative. What may be valuable to one person may not be of value to another
- Engage in mental exercises to help you address fear, uncertainty or doubt (the goal is that you approach negotiations from a place of confidence and strength)
- Identify what is key in conveying your value to a potential employer or customer
- Understand how a "worker bee or desperate jobseeker mentality" can hurt you in the negotiation process
- Identify different types of "perks" or options that may be negotiated as a part of a benefit package
- Practice techniques that will move you through the negotiations process, establishing clear understandings and "next steps"
- Prepare to onboard, asking for the "purchase order" if it is an appropriate next step (by thinking and acting like a Closer)

Temperature Check: How Comfortable Are You Addressing Your Value?

From the start of this process, it has been stressed repeatedly that this program is about identifying and leveraging *your unique value*.

- **Personal value**: This refers to the personal value that you *mindfully* offer to those you choose to enter into a relationship with (recall the "sweet 10%" who become your banner wavers discussed in Module Three).

- **Professional value**: This idea also translates to measurable professional value that you deliver to people, teams, clients and companies you work with.

Throughout this process, it is important that you actively lean into the confidence you have in the value you know you can deliver. The question is not "Can I deliver any value to this opportunity?" but rather "How much value can I deliver?" (Pause for a moment and really think about that last sentence.) We state this because there is always an amount of value you can offer almost any opportunity, no matter where you have been on the employment spectrum. From part-time or hourly, to blue collar worker to CEO, this statement is true.

In any situation (whether applying for a job, contract position or presenting your capabilities as an entrepreneurial resource) you can add some type of value no matter what you are doing. No matter whether the opportunity you have identified is at a corporate giant like Pepsi, or at a tiny start-up business, *you can add some type of value*. The only question is, how much value? Only you can determine if the opportunity you have identified is a solid fit for what excites you and is a use of your best talent.

Do you feel confident about your value? How about your value considering the subject of compensation? Some people really struggle with this notion, so it should be stressed that if you are one of these people, *it is okay*. Your rationale may stem from the notion that "employers have been good to me" so I am grateful for a paycheck. While healthy gratitude is productive, it isn't healthy if in compensation discussions your tone, body language, and demeanor come across as almost apologetic.

Mindset Matters

Two other key mindsets to be considering as it relates to compensation: the "worker-bee" mentality and, of course, as mentioned earlier in Module Two, "the desperate jobseeker" mentality. The "worker-bee" mentality is simply someone who is completely unaware of their real value. They live "paycheck to paycheck," and if combined with a "desperate jobseeker" mentality, might just do anything for the "paycheck." Worker-bee types often have a checkered employment history of jumping from job-to-job to get to bigger "paychecks." This pattern in your work history makes employers stop and pause once they recognize it. It causes them to doubt that they can change your mindset that fuels your lack of employer loyalty or sense of apparent dissatisfaction.

How do these mindsets materialize? Perhaps you never really have asked about how your work is measured, or you have a history of "just doing it." While this may be the case, it doesn't provide to you the leverage you need to explain how your unique talents deliver profits or quantified value for the company. Stated simply, you think because you show up and work hard that this entitles you to a paycheck. With the "I just want a paycheck" and worker-bee mentality you've placed the weight justifying your ask for compensation in the hands of someone who will use your last pay point, what they paid someone else, or an industry salary survey, to determine your worth.

What's tragic? Too many people operate from this perspective. It's why 80% of those employed are estimated to be "unengaged" at their job, and passively looking at other options. They are doing things they never planned on or wanted. They are not happy with their work, the company culture, or their general life direction. *Is this you?* If so, it's time you get very invested in the process because you are the *only* person who can decide "it's time to change." Here is a tough question: Do you have skin in the game? At this point do you really understand the "story of you"? Have you defined your ideal function, without relation to title or industry sector? If you have done the heavy lifting and soul searching associated with this process, you've identified something you would do every day that provides so much adrenaline that you are genuinely excited and passionate about the opportunity you have created. This ideal match you have identified should empower you to state with confidence your value. As you move to the next step, the discovery process, you will identify *exactly* how you plan to add measurable value. Have you figured this out yet? How is your mindset impacting your ability to defend your value? If you haven't done the research, or interviewed those doing what you want to do, or understood how your skills add value to companies, you must do the groundwork research, because every piece of this process compounds and builds on a previous component.

 If you are struggling, be aware that you need to *actively* work on your confidence levels because you must be intentional and clear with your ask for investment as an employee, contractor, consultant or project based hire. Mental exercises are provided at the end of this chapter to help you prepare in advance of discussions, and also to provide to your accountability group ideas on how to assist you with common challenges people have.

Another mental trap is that people frequently confuse stability with salary stating, "I need a certain level of salary to feel secure," which really is an illusion. Regarding compensation, start with defining what you believe is fair and equitable to you. What is your "definition of success" as it relates to this opportunity? You've got to have this clearly defined (as it is a key mindset) before you go into any type of salary negotiations. To get to this place, you need to do research and talk to other professionals in the role that you want. If you were in this role before, and did not feel you were fairly compensated, you need to be able to explain the gaps, and why it did not seem fair to you. You do this so that you can engineer a solution that addresses lessons you've learned, avoiding a case of "buyer's remorse." Know this, you are your own security in this process. You can't trust that the "system" will look after your interests. Ultimately you must realize that your personal and professional performance is your only true job security, not your salary.

Slow Down To Get There Faster

As discussions head toward compensation, negotiating value isn't what happens *at the end* of the process, but rather from *the first moment* you meet someone. We call this the "discovery process." During the discovery process you are identifying details (scope) of the work to be done, commitment levels and exactly what is expected. You are focusing on the question: How does my role make your company money, or add measurable value? As this process unfolds, you are building a business case for your value, framing it in terms that resonate with the decision maker. How are you accomplishing this? **You do this by constantly seeking to understand in very clear and explicit terms the expectations for how the particular job you are interested in needs to be done, and done profitably**.

Simultaneously, you are asking do I like you? Can you utilize my best talent? Do I like and fit into this culture? Am I passionate about the opportunity we are discussing? As you answer their questions, and *they answer yours*, the match emerges. But it does take time and candid dialog that goes both ways.

Remember when addressing Blues in Module Six, the idea was to "slow down to truly qualify the opportunity"? The reason for this is to make sure you understand exactly what the decision maker needs to hear (exact scope of the work) so that they are confident that you (and you alone) are uniquely qualified to deliver this value based on your experiences. You can only accomplish this goal if you talk openly about how their expectations and your experiences align.

This idea really cannot be stressed enough because it is mission critical that both parties have clear and well-defined expectations for the business measures and outcomes "associated with success" in the role, project or position. If you have held a similar position in the past, *you may want to skip this step*. You might assume that you and the person (or team) you are speaking with hold similar "definitions of success," or notions of how a job should be done. In efforts to be polite or sensitive to time, you may want to talk high level about details, but do not skip this critical step of confirming details and understandings.

Dive Deep

Should this employer or client have different measures for a successful outcome, don't skip past pesky details like specific problems that need to be solved (within a certain timeframe), or key performance indicators (KPI's), by making unconfirmed assumptions. **Take time to ask what the company or team's strategic plan calls for as it relates to measurable outcomes associated with the role or project**. You need to ask in specific terms how the role, project, or opportunity is anticipated to make the company money or deliver value. **If the people to whom you are speaking can't answer this question, then you are probably not speaking to the right person or decision maker.** Or, what's worse, is that they may not have considered this issue (which often presents *at minimum* a need for clarification).

Why ask these questions? You need to ask prior to a negotiation so you know how to position your value and frame the logic behind your ask.

You must have a mutually understood vocabulary as it relates to "measures for success" associated with the job or opportunity at hand. Ask probing questions that help you to understand the scope and requirements of the job (role or projects). Then, once you have a clear understanding, thank them for the level of detail they provided, and ask if you can forward to them detailed case studies, examples or illustrations (your value proposition) that further demonstrate how you have solved similar problems and crafted solutions referencing other clients, employers, or projects you've worked.

Whether you accomplish this goal in a single setting, or through *several* talks with department leaders or teams, at every interface you are looking to identify and confirm aligned expectations about specific value you will deliver. Once you have identified the expectations of each individual as it relates to your hiring, send a note that reiterates that you have heard their priorities. With this note, and a sincere thank you, you attach your value proposition (customized case studies) that illustrate how you have accomplished this in the past. Still struggling? Please review the different types of value proposition case studies that are available as handouts associated with this module.

Talking Ballpark Sooner Than Later

If provided an opportunity, the question of your value as it relates to "ballpark" estimates for salary range or project fees should come up *quickly* or *early* in process so that no one wastes their time. Too often people tread lightly about fees, project budgets, or salary. There is no reason to do so if you are at the appropriate place in the conversation to bring up the subject of ballpark estimates for the work that needs to be done.

It is also time for you to identify deal killers. Deal killers are things that must be included in an offer or agreement that are "non-negotiables." Deal killers might include less than three weeks' vacation, 50% travel, aggressive production deadlines, or payment terms. What things are negotiable or non-negotiable for you? Now is the time to make the list. As you think about package offers for employment, the offer might include a broad spectrum of items such as:

- Vacation

- Education or Ongoing Professional Certification Incentives

- Exit Strategy (if you leave)

- Car or Travel Benefits

- Health Benefits

- Signing or Performance Bonuses

Once you have in your mind your needs concerning compensation, and things are "humming along" in the interview and rapport building process, it's important that you "gut check" your own level of enthusiasm as it relates to the culture of the company, the people to whom you will be working, or with and the actual job you will do. Now is the time to ask, "Do I really want this and is it a good fit?" because *any* reservations you have are worth thinking through in detail *before* you talk ball park salary ranges. Have you ever ignored your gut feelings? In the long term, how did it ultimately work out? You need to pay attention to how you feel when you are in the company, or with the team you would be working. If you sense dread, lack of enthusiasm, numbness, or a genuine lack of connection, you need to pay attention and back off continued conversations.

If you have no serious reservations, then you need to ask about ballpark salary or project ranges to make sure that your "definition of your price *aligns* with their expectation of value."

Getting In The Ballpark

You do this by squarely positioning your value (or fee structure) against the required outcomes associated with role or project, asking the question, "does this role/project pay in the ball park of $X?" or "what is your budget range for the work proposed?" A general formula to keep in mind is that you need to be making nearly a million dollar contribution to offset a salary and benefits package equivalent to $125K. Should they be unable to get to your preferred salary or project compensation range, questions you can use to further open the dialog as you go through the discovery process might include:

- When I hit a certain % of revenue or production goal, while you might not have the funds today, may I have the money then?

- Can you pay retroactively when I hit this revenue number or deliver this value point? What is the best way to structure compensation?

Once these questions are presented, if the role or project budget is not a match for your qualifications, then it is time to politely draw the conversation to a close. Perhaps you can refer them to a provider or know of an individual that is more aligned with their budget.

Keep in mind that while they may say "they can't afford your rate or salary range," should the *opportunity fit be exceptional*, you may want to get creative in how they can hire or engage you. You may ask, "if I can demonstrate exceptional value, or I could do more to add measurable value to the position, can you be more flexible with the salary range, or can you create a new position?" Should they be unable to accomplish your ballpark range because at this time they just don't have the funds, then leave the door open for later discussions. Indicate that, should circumstances change, they can call you later (this often happens with corporations once you have had several solid interviews and you are on file as a highly qualified candidate).

If they are a smaller firm that cannot meet your salary range...

- Perhaps they can then pay you in a creative combination of cash, equity or options?

- Maybe through a performance bonus?

- Through commissions on revenue that you bring to the table?

- Perhaps your value is through delivering valuable strategic partnerships?

- Or you have relationships and connections you can bring to the table that will open access to new markets?

There are many ways to get creative about compensation, but the value for both parties is relative to the person to whom it is being offered. So maybe they can't afford you full time, but you could do a project for them. Don't fail to try to get creative if it's a great match.

Is The Offer Fair?

Rather than asking if the deal is "fair," why not ask how the deal/offer/package makes you *feel*? Only then can you determine if what you have negotiated as a package is fair. *Why?* Because value is extremely relative. What might be a good fit for one person may be a bad fit (or feel "unfair") for another.

Frequently the question arises in negotiations, "I've been offered $X for the job, project or role, is this fair market value?" An industry salary survey might address this question one way (what the industry pays for this role), but we would argue that what a generic salary survey suggests is *vaguely* defined at best. While a marketing manager might historically be paid $42.5K, the real issue is how you feel about the value associated with the offer, and how that value aligns against measurable value you can deliver.

Dollars And Sense

When an entrepreneurial mindset is in motion during this process, you are typically selling your value as a consultant, project manager or service solution provider. This is when thinking "like a Closer" requires that you know how to strongly position price as it relates to value. While we never suggest that you "do work cheaply" (your reputation is *everything*), you need to understand that sometimes this is a mindset of some decision makers (they have champagne taste on a beer budget). If you encounter this, hopefully you have already addressed their definition of value as it relates to price *early* in the process of discussing an opportunity.

If you have not talked about price, value, and fit, let's illustrate the idea through an exercise that may help you to identify pricing criteria. Stop and consider what people typically want when they buy things. They want the project done very well, perhaps very fast or very cheaply. Typically, any one of these types of descriptors might provide a market advantage. Considering these three things, choose two that describe what the decision maker has said is important. The only rule is that they can only choose two of three options that will impact priority and pricing: fast, good or cheap. The following combinations describe how you might approach pricing, avoiding the pitfall of misaligned value and price:

Good and Fast = More expensive pricing. Choose good and fast, and other opportunity options might be pushed out of the priority line. You put top priority on the work at hand by moving quick, which means that most likely you can price higher because you are providing this opportunity high priority and access.

Good and Cheap = If this combination surfaces, it suggests that you need to do a good job at the work requested for a lesser price if their budget does not accommodate your normal fee structure. However, in managing the buyer expectations, they will need to be patient (or flexible) in the delivery process or timeline because other work will need to take priority due to financial risks.

Fast and Cheap = If the buyer gravitates this direction, they are asking you to sacrifice the quality of the work to deliver what most likely will be an inferior job quickly. This doesn't make sense for either party.

Putting The Ideal Process Together

From the beginning of this course we've been emphasizing the importance of managing expectations and building relationships based on mutual respect. If you've been following the process to this point, you've done a number of things to properly position your value, while operating from a place of strength with those that you are pursuing relationships. First, you have been carefully evaluating how the story of you is a meaningful match for the opportunity you have identified. In this you have discovered an alignment and "good fit" between what you want to do and skills or outcomes that this particular opportunity requires.

Second, you've done extensive research on the company and/or industry. You have identified and spent time with the decision maker. You have asked about the work or role in enough detail to understand the strategic outcomes that the hiring party hopes to achieve (the measures of success associated with the role or outcome of the work you will perform). You have expressed a solid interest in and discussed how in the past your unique skills and best talents have been used to solve challenges or address situations such as this to create measurable impact. At every interaction you are reflecting as to whether there is a genuine "love connection" or cultural fit between you and the employer or client.

In connecting, you have established solid communications with the person who understands the requirements of the role. You have shared with them the "story of you," and have effectively positioned your value by explaining to them how your "best talent" (or value proposition) can address the measurable need(s) that the company has. Measurable needs include things like increased market share, improved or diversified vendors, better purchasing terms, more efficient internal processes designed to eliminate overhead or create new pockets of customer value, market opportunity, competitive value, industry innovation, or other benefits for the company. If you have listened carefully to what the company says it needs, and have applied what you have learned, you have the details you need to squarely align your best talent against the *mutually understood* requirements of the opportunity in case studies customized to illustrate this value. You are prepared and positioned to identify specific performance expectations (or estimate requirements associated with the opportunity) so that you can frame the parameters of value you plan to deliver around the scope that the company needs to address.

Closing Strategies

When you get to the time to close the deal, you need to clearly *express interest* and *clearly ask* for the opportunity. You need to say that you would like an offer or ask to put together a proposal. You need to state that you feel this is a fit and would like the opportunity to work with them. You can accomplish this by asking the simple question, "is there any reason you wouldn't hire me?"

In closing, you need to pick a style of communication that is best for the person to whom you are appealing. You need to do what will work for you in a way that aligns with the preference of the person that is the decision maker. If they prefer a phone call, phone them to ask for the job. If they are "meet in person" type, ask to meet with them in person. If you have someone who likes emails and defers meetings, email them to ask for the opportunity, or even text them (if this is their preference) once all of the discovery process hurdles have been addressed, and it's a natural place in the process to do so.

If you have sent your value propositions and case studies to your internal contacts, and have discussed price or elements of the compensation package, it's time to close the deal by deciding you do indeed want to engage one another. What is a great way to do this? You may want to ask for a "war room" planning session to layout priorities for on-boarding and parameters for a 30/60/90 day performance plan. This is "not another interview," but a collaboration to make sure that everyone has the same information and expectations associated with the process. In this you need to be comfortable presenting your plans for the role (or project), what needs to get done (KPI's), and how you plan to do what needs to be done profitably. The beauty of a 30/60/90 day plan is that you know exactly the measures that will be used to determine the quality of your performance during the trial period. When you do this, it can make a tremendous impact on the quality of the offer because everyone gets focused in the same direction. You get clarity on exactly how you will be measured and there is a definition of "mutual success." You can reconfirm everything you know, simply taking it a step deeper. Often, you will identify new variables or risks during the process that will help you add clarity in your discussions on compensation. Instead of having an employment contract just handed to you with terms defined, you can be a part of the process, establishing terms and conditions associated with how you will be measured and prepared to participate in these measures. What has been observed in this process is that offers can increase by significant numbers. Different roles may emerge because of "better fits" for your capabilities (usually more substantial roles), or you might be offered a "lesser role" because the position appears to be past your capabilities.

What can happen? Everyone may confirm we are on the same page and good to go. Or, there may be a "hey, we need to slow down as there are issues we weren't aware of." You may also hear "we didn't think about that, we need to consider this," or "we couldn't be further apart." The "we couldn't be further apart" may not be something you want to hear, but wouldn't you rather hear it now then be set-up for failure because there was no alignment of expectations from the beginning? Nobody wants buyer's remorse. The value of this planning session is that it clarifies expectations for performance reviews, while positioning you to on-board assuming no last minute disconnects.

Exercise 1: Haste Makes Waste

Think about a time where you pushed for or got into a job or project commitment too quickly. What caused this experience? What types of emotions or mindsets may have contributed to things moving too quickly? What were you afraid of in the interview process or what did you want to avoid? What did this experience teach you about yourself? Reflecting on this situation, what can you take away and apply to where you are at today? Prepare to discuss what happened to you and how you felt about it with your accountability partners. Ask them: Does this seem like a mistake I'd make today? Can you see how I might behave this way? What do you think causes me to agree to jobs or work that is a poor fit? (Are there attitudes I have that surface when I'm unaware? Behaviors I almost "unconsciously" engage in or skills I lack?)

Exercise 2: Getting Into Your Most Confident Mindset

Think of a time you were your most satisfied and happy both personally and professionally. This is the person that you want to be, especially at the negotiating table. As you think about the task at hand in negotiating your compensation, don't focus on the end result (a number). Rather focus on the things that you need to communicate in a specific sequence to justify that number. As you reflect on the conversation you will have, play it out mentally. How do you *feel* as you imagine the situation?

If you feel "fear of loss" this is something to identify and deal with *before* you get into the negotiations. It can be something that has surfaced in your life in other ways, perhaps you just don't recognize it. Are you afraid of asking for raises? Have you avoided compensation discussions because of fear, uncertainty and doubt? If so, most likely it's a problem you've carried your entire work experience, this just might be the first time you are becoming truly aware of it.

When you are your most happy and contented self, you are not motivated by fear. You have peace of mind because you can trust yourself, you are the one making the decisions and at the helm. This is the person that you need to be, because when you can tap this mindset and you've combined it with logic to support your value, you are not being demeaned or fearing rejection. You are prepared to have a well-structured and logic-driven discussion that is based in confidence.

The more confident you become in preparation, the less susceptible you are to negative influences, attitudes, mindsets or behaviors. Your goal before critical talks occur is to practice your ask with your accountability group. You need to be intentional by exploring your mindsets, practicing the art of being your most confident and authentic self.

Exercise 3: Practice Makes Perfect

As you continue to reflect on your most confident self, is there anything that has changed that keeps you from being "that most confident and authentic person"? If so, how can you overcome these barriers? You were once there, how can you take actions to "get back"? What would make you feel more confident? Ask your accountability partners that you trust, where you can improve in the areas of confidence and sincerity.

Ask:

- When we discuss compensation, how is my body language? Closed, open? Relaxed, uptight?

- Eye contact?

- Behavior cues?

- Am I consistent or inconsistent in the way I present myself? What could improve? How could I be more consistent or demonstrate more confidence?

- Are there non-threatening situations that can I apply or practice what I'm learning about myself in the next week? Will I commit to practicing these skills, reporting back on my progress?

Keep Your YBR Updated By Managing Your Reds That Become Greens

Once you have a Red opportunity that has made a "yes or no" decision, the relationship is evergreen or "Green." If the opportunity is a "go," then you need to prepare to do project start-up, or on-board.

If it is a no, then write a note of thank you wishing them the best with their new hire or vendor. Plan a follow-up in about 2-4 weeks to see how things are going and simply to say hello. Why do this? You may find that keeping in touch, should things with the other person not work out, you are back at the table, or in line for future work where they think you would be a great fit because there was so much positive conclusion in their experience with you. Also, at this point you are very invested in the relationship. For whatever reason you were not a good fit at this time for them, they may know of a company they can refer you to that may make a next great step for you.

Accountability Meeting Agenda

:00 Review

- [ ] Reflect on the exercises, share with your partners how they challenged you
- [ ] Major events, opportunities and interviews
- [ ] Schedule time with each other to practice closing strategies and to review structure for negotiations

:15 Discuss

- [ ] Your MAP
- [ ] Your YBR
- [ ] Your next steps to convert Yellows to Blues

:35 Homework

- [ ] Contact five Whites for opportunities
- [ ] Deadline:

- [ ] How you will score success:
- [ ] Follow-up with contacts from previous weeks
- [ ] Deadline:
- [ ] How you will score success:
- [ ] Schedule time with one another to practice final interview, closing techniques, or mindset exercises

:55 *Scoring and Closing Encouragement*

- [ ] Score your efforts from this past week
- [ ] End with encouragement

Assignments for Next Session

- [ ] Read Module Nine: On-Boarding
- [ ] Practice mindfulness as it relates to confidence mindsets and being your most authentic self
- [ ] Meet with your accountability partners
- [ ] Review your MAP and YBR progress: Is your MAP updated? Are call back dates and next steps clear? What does your YBR say about your ability to move opportunities through a pipeline? What do the colors tell you about behaviors or skills you need to work on? (Too many Yellows? Maybe you are busy but unproductive, if none of the people are meeting with are qualified to discuss a true opportunity, moving a Yellow to a Blue. Too many Reds? Are you being selective and honest about what you are applying for, retrofitting yourself into everything? Are you "stuck" in any way? What actions or alterations to your approach can you take to get "unstuck" or try things differently to get to more productive results?)
- [ ] Contact five Whites for opportunities, keep in touch with your banner wavers
- [ ] In thinking about your progress to date, what patterns are you seeing? How can you constructively make progress against the attitudes that might be holding you back, behaviors that are unproductive or skills you need help in developing? Create a plan to set goals and ask your accountability group to help you make weekly progress by taking small doable steps

Module Nine: On-Boarding

Objectives
By the end of this module, you will:

- Know how to make this process as seamless as possible for each party, whether you are acting as a contractor, employee or entrepreneur
- Identify steps to be proactive in the process
- Become accountable for this activity (as some companies have no formalized process)
- Identify paperwork you can provide to accelerate the process
- Identify meetings you should participate in
- Determine if you should ask for an opportunity to "shadow"
- Manage relations in a positive way to reinforce the idea of "no surprises" moving forward
- Understand that there is value in again confirming your assumptions in advance of "starting work"

Make It Easy By Being Proactive
Once a yes or no decision has been made, if you are on-boarding or doing a project start up as a contractor service provider, you should be proactive about the process. Why be proactive? Because many times companies lack a formalized on-boarding process. How do you be proactive? Begin by asking who you should contact in HR to begin the process of accepting an offer and on-boarding. Realize, if it is a small company, they may have no one formally in this role, so be sensitive to the size of company you are dealing with.

To the degree you can have your paperwork done, or accelerate the process before you start, try to do so. If joining a larger company, realize that they typically have a set of steps that help you to understand legal risks, benefits and non-competes. These steps are designed to defer risk for the large company, but don't necessarily benefit you. What would benefit you is to ask between now and the time you start, is there anything I can do to hit the ground running on day one? Anything you can do will make the process easier for everyone. If there's a request that should be made, do make it.

Shadow If Possible
Should you have three weeks before a start date, ask if there is anyone you can shadow for a day or two to get to know the ropes. The experience will give you an insider view of culture and help you to understand a bit about "water cooler" culture and internal processes. Also, ask about any meetings that might be important for you to attend prior to your start date. *Why do this?* So that you show initiative and shake the "new person" label, being in position to bond well with your new teammates. Simply, the more you show your excitement to be there, the more impressed the people will be that made the decision to hire you. Plus, you get to see closer how people really interact with one another. Essentially you have seen previews of the movie up to this point, now

you get to look closer before you join the cast of characters which can help you gain further insights before you start. The key advantage with this is that the ice is broken before you start. You have a chance to forge an impression before you get there, and you should take the opportunity. Also, if you come from a bigger corporate background, and you are joining a small firm or even a start-up, you need to be ready for culture shock. Anything you can do to prepare yourself is helpful.

Don't Underestimate The Value of Bonding

If you can go out to dinner with your team and new boss before you arrive, do join them for dinner with your spouse. Spend some time with your teammates, go on a sales call, do whatever you can to show an availability and an interest in bonding with people personally and professionally. Why? Because it makes all the difference in setting the tone for your next experience.

If You Are A Contractor Or Service Provider

Now is the time to really accelerate expectation management. Spend time up front on confirming scope of the work. Confirm the timelines for production, details about production, or your anticipated billing sequence. Send to the accounting department or purchasing your employer number and tax forms so they can prepare to process your invoices.

This is the time to demonstrate to the decision maker that they've made an excellent decision in hiring you, and you do that by making the process of doing business with you simple and as seamless as possible.

Exercise 1: Are You Ready To On-board?

Make a to do list of items you need to have on hand to provide to HR or purchasing. Make sure these items are available to the person who will guide the process, by proactively reaching out to them and requesting a meeting for the purpose of on-boarding.

_____

_____

_____

Exercise 2: Manage Your Time Well

If you've been unemployed or in transition for some time, and you are headed back to a full-time job, prepare yourself in advance by waking up at a proper time at least a week before you start back to work. Review your wardrobe. Are you prepared to go back into an office environment? Dress for the job you want, not for the one you might have. If you need to get clothes dry-cleaned and pressed, and shoes polished, do so to start out well. Also, drive the route to work before you go so that you know at the rush hour what traffic is really like, and what parking you have available. Too often we hear horror stories of new hires who arrive an hour late to work on their first day because they had no idea of where to park, which only makes you look incompetent.

Exercise 3: Open Q & A

Ask your group members for help and advice with problems.

- Where are you stuck?

_____

_____

_____

- On the other hand, what is working well?

_____

_____

_____

Keep Working Your YBR

Reminder: Keep pursuing other opportunities, even if you have Reds. Too often people think something is "closed" or a "done deal" when it is not, and during the process, you may have neglected other viable options by focusing too much on one thing.

Color	Next Step Deadline	Next Step	Opportunity	Contact	Notes
Red	7/7	**Tell Larry my final decision**	EZRecs – PT Biller	Larry Young	**7/6 Offered FT job** 6/12 Interviewed 6/9 Email exchange
Red	7/9	**2nd interview**	Emerald, Inc – Biller	Oscar Diggs	**6/24 Met w/Oscar, 2nd mtg on 7/9** 6/7 Call

Accountability Meeting Agenda

:00 Review

- ☐ Major events
- ☐ Homework (contact five people, YBR follow-ups)

:15 Discuss

- ☐ Your MAP
- ☐ Your YBR
- ☐ Your next steps to convert Blues to Reds, stay focused on Blues and Yellows even while trying to close Reds (you never want your pipeline to be empty or stagnant)

:35 Homework

- ☐ Contact five Whites for opportunities
- ☐ Deadline:
- ☐ How you will score success:
- ☐ Follow-up with contacts and banner wavers from previous weeks
- ☐ Deadline:
- ☐ How you will score success:

:55 Scoring and Closing Encouragement

- ☐ Score your efforts from this past week
- ☐ End with encouragement

Assignments

- ☐ Read Module Ten: Welcome To A New Way Of Life
- ☐ Meet with your accountability partner
- ☐ Review your MAP and YBR progress
- ☐ Contact five Whites for opportunities
- ☐ Keep looking for Yellows. Work to convert them to Blues (and Blues to Reds)
- ☐ Reflect on how far you've come, and do something special to celebrate your personal progress

Module Ten: Welcome To A New Way Of Life

MAP
Approach
Prospect Pool

Generate
Yellow Leads
Prospector

Follow Up Post-
Sale, Greens
Get Referrals

Qualify Blue Leads
Initial Interview
Technical Expert

Sales Pitch, Red Leads
In-Person Interview
Closer

Objectives

- Know how to get the most out of every outcome, even if it's a no
- Be ready to drive your long-term career with what matters most in life: relationships
- Realize the dangers in "getting too comfortable"
- Recognize excuses that are common once you "get a job"
- Realize the value of modeling these mindsets, and skills for others that might be looking to you to help them
- Realize anyone can "do this process"
- Recognize what you can control and what you can't, deciding on the ongoing path that's best for you to keep your options open

Evergreen: Perennial Contacts

When you reach the final result of an opportunity, convert it—and its associated relationships—to Green. Relationships last longer than just one Red opportunity. They are Evergreen!

Every YBR opportunity is a chance to form new, lasting relationships. Keep cultivating these new Greens even when the opportunity did not work out.

Post-Opportunity Checklist

- ☐ Get feedback from the interviewer
- ☐ Debrief with accountability partner
- ☐ Thank people you met along the way
- ☐ Make an introduction
- ☐ Keep options open for the future

Get Feedback from the Decision Maker

When it was still a Blue, you asked the interviewer to give you feedback at the end. When you hear the result, what questions can you ask to get the feedback you need to grow?

Accountability Partner Debrief

Go over the entire experience. What can you learn from it? Get their honest opinion. Ask for help identifying strengths to play on, and weaknesses to improve.

Exercise 1: Debrief Practice

With a partner, do a mini-debrief of your most recent interview experience. If you have not had an interview, debrief a recent pre-interview conversation (5 min each), and brainstorm the art of follow-up.

Remember: Write a thank-you note to every person you met along the way. This is your chance to create a friend and to keep options open for the future.

Introduce a Friend

- If you got the job, how can you leverage this for others' benefit?
- Who can you introduce?
- Can you subcontract any of your work?
- Even if you did not get the job, do they have any opportunities you could tell others about, or help them fill through relationships in your network?

Regularly reach out to your network about opportunities they are seeking.

Keep Options Open for the Future

Relationships are your bread and butter—don't let them grow stale. Don't burn bridges when the result is a no. Another opportunity with them might later end up a yes.

Once you accept an offer, inform your other opportunities (Reds and Blues). It is professional, resolves loose ends, and builds relationships. But don't assume you have the job until the papers are signed!

Update your MAP with Evergreens:
- MAP = a habit regardless of whether you're looking for work

The more people you know, the more opportunities you can connect to, and the more valuable you will be.

Exercise 2: Cultivate Relationships

In groups of three, list ways to:

- Do post-opportunity follow-up

_____

_____

_____

- Stay in touch with your relationships and banner wavers over the long-term

_____

_____

_____

The End? Not Quite. Think Marathon, Not Sprint

Short-term might be straight forward. It is a thank-you note, a call or an invite. How do you build a long-term foundation of real relationships? Know that it takes planning, energy, attention and engagement. (This doesn't just accidentally "happen"). **Shift must happen within and it must be a permanent shift for it to be considered a successful shift.** Why? Because layoffs also happen. Typical transition is a 12-18 month cycle that rarely can be avoided unless you are ready and prepared. The Economy Of One mindset, tools and processes will keep you prepared for any "shift" should it happen unexpectedly.

While you might land in a comfortable situation, don't get comfortable. Things can and often do happen. Too frequently it's reported "I quit this process when I got a job. I just got so busy that continuing to meet people and expand my relationships didn't make sense, so I stopped."

Well, stop and think about this…

You need to remember how you feel being at the mercy of a system that has reduced you to a piece of paper. Remember what it is like not to pay your mortgage or to feel insecure. Too often, once you go through the process, it's easy to go right back to your old ways of thinking, to treat people as a means to an end, and to ignore the very relationships that delivered the opportunity to your doorstep. People stop the behavior of meeting new people and being intentional about adding "personal and professional value" to everyone they meet, because they are suddenly "just too busy to think about it anymore." Don't be one of these very short-sighted people!

This takes effort and intentionality in moving forward. You have got to continue to make the effort so that you never find yourself without opportunities again. *The flat-out truth?* If you aren't willing to make and maintain the effort, there's nothing else we can do for you because we can lead you to water, but we cannot make you drink. Keep in mind that when you model this behavior for your children, explaining why you are doing what you are doing, and even inviting them to be your accountability helpers, your kids will follow your example. You will help them to see what they need to do to nurture relationships, be kindhearted personally and feel empowered professionally instead of entitled. The entire family benefits from your discipline, and thinks and behaves differently.

This could be compared to weight loss. Once you hit your goal weight, then what? For too many, this is when they quit. They go back to Doritos and Ding Dongs and wonder what happened. "Slim for Life" became "Slim for Now" and they neglect the *very thing* that delivered wild success. You must look at "here forward" in the same way as maintaining a weight goal. You'll have to continue to work for it.

And is it worth working for? *YES!* Your career choices and income earning opportunities in life make every other decision more meaningful. If you stay focused, you never again have to draft a meaningless document with a bunch of words that determine your future and post it "out there," crossing your fingers hoping for the best. Rather, maintain control over what you can control (your attitudes, behaviors and skills). Let go of serving a system that was never designed to serve your interests in the first place, and decide that you will never leave things to a piece of paper, put in the hands of others who are not vested in your success.

Stay true to the relationships that are always the lifeline to revenue. United, we stand. Divided, we fall. **You are an Economy Of One!** Join others in our alumni group and join the rapidly expanding group of others who share your values (the sweet 10%) by registering online at EconomyOfOne.com

Accountability Meeting Agenda (Future Meetings)

:00 *Review*

☐ Major events

☐ Stop as a group and think back to the beginning and how far you've collectively come. Compliment one another for a specific area of growth you've observed

:15 *Discuss*

☐ Your YBR

☐ Your MAP

☐ Homework

☐ Deadline

☐ How you will score success

:55 *Scoring and Closing Encouragement*

☐ Score your efforts from this past week

☐ End with encouragement

☐ Plan your next update

Final Q & A: THE ECONOMY OF ONE Troubleshooting

What final questions or concerns do you have about THE ECONOMY OF ONE?

_____

_____

_____

What's changed in your life through this experience? What do you do differently?

_____

_____

_____

What have you learned about yourself?

_____

_____

_____

Concluding Participant Survey

Please complete the survey in the back of the workbook.

Great Reading Resources

- Necessary Endings by Dr. Henry Cloud
- Failing Forward: Turning Mistakes Into Stepping Stones for Success by John Maxwell
- Go Givers Sell More by Bob Burg and John David Mann
- Battlefield of the Mind by Joyce Meyer

Coming Soon: The Economy Of One App

We will have a technology that automates many MAP and YBR tasks, helping you stay easily organized. It's like a relational Fitbit. Stay tuned for when this is available at EconomyOfOne.com

Extra Credit:

Create Your Brand

Objectives

By the end of this unit, you will:

- Know how companies use human brands to build group identity and purchase loyalty.
- Have your own personal brand.
- Be able to test and improve it.

Introduction

Rule #1: People do business with people they like and trust.

Your brand is how you foster likability and trust. How do you represent yourself every day? This includes dress, habits, attitudes, etc.

Brands Build Relationships and Trust

Who would *you* trust with your business? Appearance matters more than you think.

Human vs. Personal Branding

- Human branding—You represent a company and its identity, values and image.
- Personal branding—You represent yourself and your identity, values and image.

What is Human Branding?

It's powerful magic. It can create lifelong financial habits, reshape values, and create or destroy alliances between people. British scientists used brain scans to show that some people's loyalty to Apple is equivalent to a religious experience.[1]

Businesses use employees to influence customers into sharing the brand's identity and values.

- Example: Oprah

---

[1] Yin, Sara. "Apple Provides Fans With Religious Experience, Brain Scans Reveal." *PCMAG.* 17 May 2011. Web. 5 June 2015.

Exercise 1: Your Favorite Brand

Think of one brand you feel loyal to.

- What values does it represent to you?

_____

_____

- What emotions do you feel when you think of the brand or its products?

_____

_____

_____

What is Personal Branding?

It is doing individually the branding that corporations do collectively. You display:

- Who you are?
- What you represent?
- What you can do for them?

You infuse your brand in everything you do:

- Dress, appearance, mannerisms, personality
- Communication styles, online presence
- History, reputation, relationships, interactions
- What you do and promise to do?

Why Have a Brand?

Your brand can distinguish you from competitors who are just as qualified. Your brand is for life—not just employers!

Branding is a sniff test about trust. People need to experience your brand to decide what to do with you. "Do our two brands align in values, promises and personality?"

Branding Goes Both Ways

Research the brands of whomever you want to do business with.

- Who are they?
- What are their values?

Exercise 2: Identify Client Brands

Consider the companies or types of clients you would like to have hire you.

- What are the elements of their brand?

_____

_____

_____

- What kinds of products, services and values do their brands represent?

_____

_____

_____

- How do their brands align with your vision for your *Economy of One?*

_____

_____

_____

Offline Personal Branding

It is your relationships, image, attire and habits. One THE ECONOMY OF ONE participant wrote, "In the age of dressing down, I break away from the pack—and it shows."

Exercise 3: Social Skills

How are your social skills? Ask your accountability partner to be straightforward and challenge you in this. Where can you improve? (One idea: Up your game in thanking people for helping you network!)

- One thing you do well socially:

_____

_____

_____

- One thing you can improve:

_____

_____

_____

Online Personal Branding

People use social networks to judge who you know. Companies hire people for their connections not just their skills.

Exercise 4: Your Online Brand

- What does your online presence say about your brand and your network?

_____

_____

_____

Exercise 5: Create Your Brand

Use what you learned last week and include values, skills, passions, vision and the main purpose and value you create. "This is who I present to the world."

- What central promise do you want to make through your brand to potential clients or employers?

_____

_____

_____

- What value do you want to create for others?

_____

_____

_____

Exercise 6: Implement Your Brand

List three steps to take this week to better convey your brand in your everyday life:

1.

_____

2.

_____

3.

_____

Summarize your brand in ten words or less. This is your Personal Brand Tagline:

_____

_____

_____

Exercise 7: Test Your Brand

With a partner, test your brand. In one minute, describe who you are and what you do, and then share your tagline.

Partners, share three ways their style and demeanor affirm or undermine their brand. Be kind, honest and constructive!

1.

_____

2.

_____

3.

_____

Accountability Meeting Agenda

:00 Review

- ☐ Major events
- ☐ Homework (contact five people for opportunities)

:15 Discuss

- ☐ Your personal brand
- ☐ Ways to implement it (Ex. 6)
- ☐ Feedback from others (Ex. 7)

:35 Homework

- ☐ Implement your personal brand
- ☐ Deadline:
- ☐ How you will score success:
- ☐ Contact five people for opportunities
- ☐ Deadline:
- ☐ How you will score success:

:55 Scoring and closing encouragement

- ☐ Score your efforts from this past week
- ☐ End with encouragement

Assignments for Next Session

- ☐ Meet with your accountability partner
- ☐ Implement your personal brand
- ☐ Put your Tagline where you will see it daily
- ☐ Contact five people for opportunities
- ☐ Bring your contact list to class next week

Participant Survey

Circle stars to rate the following components. Feel free to add comments.

☆ ☆ ☆ ☆ ☆   PowerPoint presentations

☆ ☆ ☆ ☆ ☆   Participant Workbook

☆ ☆ ☆ ☆ ☆   *The Economy of One* reading materials

☆ ☆ ☆ ☆ ☆   Homework assignments (putting THE ECONOMY OF ONE into practice)

☆ ☆ ☆ ☆ ☆   Accountability Partner experience

What did we do best?

What can we do to improve?

How have your results in looking for work changed since starting THE ECONOMY OF ONE?

How has your perspective about yourself and your career changed?

List of Definitions

Terminology	Definition
30/60/90 Day Plan	These are key productivity indicators (KPI's) that companies should have defined pre-hire to determine the productivity measures associated with the role under consideration. KPI's are important to have defined so that an individual can meet and exceed expectations associated with the job, role, or project.
4th Most Important Decision	There are four critical decisions you make in life. 1. Do you believe in God? 2. Do you marry or not? 3. Do you try to have kids or not? 4. What do you do with your time on planet earth? We call the fourth question a most important question in life because if you get it right, the other three questions become much easier to answer and enjoy.
Accountability Group	A group of people who are invested and "present" for your support and development. You are in a weekly relationship with them where you report progress toward your goals. They are objective, positive, and committed to your success. They help you address attitudes, behaviors, and skills that will assure your success. They pray for you (if you desire it), help you make decisions, and are looking for ways to actively support you in your journey to become an Economy of One. They are a safe place for you to park emotions or experiences that are detrimental. They are people you can always call that will do all in their power to help you and they can count on you to reciprocate.
Addendum	Documents that are submitted throughout the interviewing process as you learn more about how you will create value. These documents are a supplement to your original thank-you on steroids. Helpful when it is time to negotiate compensation. These documents will also allow you to leave behind a great footprint for future reference.
Bad Boss	Someone who espouses values, skills, attitudes, or behaviors that they do not embody.
Ballpark Number	A number you would use when estimating a project fee, a fee for engagement, or base salary within communications resulting in further negotiation.

Terminology	Definition
Banner Wavers	People you know and have an ongoing relationship with who advocate actively on your behalf amongst their friends and connections. They know the "story of you," can position your value and are committed to your success. They actively make introductions on your behalf and help you to position your value in the marketplace.
Benefits	A list of completely negotiable terms that address tangible and intangible perks associated with employment.
Best Talent	Your "best talents" are the skills you most enjoy using. They often add the most value to those you serve. They are the skills that define or anchor you professionally.
Call Reluctance	The incorrect tendency to believe that when reaching out to others you are "bothering them." It results in "inertia and no activity." It is a false belief that the act of contacting others is an inconvenience to them. The truth is that in connecting with others, you provide an opportunity to be of service.
Chamber Of Commerce	Most cities have a local or regional membership group known as the Chamber of Commerce. These are representative companies and their employees who meet regularly to discuss business issues relevant to the local or regional community.
Closer	The entrepreneurial mindset, skill, behavior required by an individual to negotiate terms and conditions, to close an opportunity. They have both the ability and authority (line item negotiation) to finalize the terms of a professional engagement.
Compensation	A broad term that encompasses what is negotiable in business engagement. It may include obvious things like pay, PTO, vacation days, or a car. Compensation may also cover intangibles like terms associated with a non-compete agreement or an exit clause.
Connector	A person who holds the intent and mindset to create value for others by actively making introductions on their behalf. They follow through and actively deliver new relationship opportunities, building trust amongst their peers. The purpose of each introduction is for mutual value.

Terminology	Definition
Contractor vs. Employee	A contractor is an individual hired for a specific job, project, or amount of agreed-upon time. An employee works part or fulltime for a company. By definition, an employee has vastly different tax and HR implications than a contractor.
Corporate Culture	Companies, like people, have personalities. Each department often assumes the personality of its people and leadership. Corporate culture describes the personality of a company. When considering employment options, corporate culture is the top consideration because if people don't genuinely like each other, nothing else matters; it won't work!
Customizing Communication	The act of providing "meaningful" written or oral details specific to the scope of the opportunity (the work that needs to be done) that you are pursuing. It might include customization of a resume, bio, addendum, or work portfolio.
Decision Maker	The person who has the authority to hire, buy, or write a check.
Desperate Jobseeker	A mindset and set of "desperate" behaviors displayed by those who are desperate to find a "job." This mindset demeans and dehumanizes the process of employment and makes people feel helpless.
Direct to Companies	When a person goes "direct to companies" they seek to establish communications with the decision-makers and/or gatekeepers.
Discovery Meeting	A meeting designed to raise questions around the scope of the work required for any job or project, and requirements associated with the work or project being discussed.
Document Trail	Written or electronic communications associated with personal communications associated with the application or presentation for work, contract, or creation of opportunity.
Due Diligence	To intentionally review details or references associated with the job or opportunity to determine if indeed it is a good fit for both parties. Mutual value is the goal.
E-mail Agenda	A document that identifies in priority the purpose(s) and topic(s) to be addressed at the meeting.
Executive Agent	A person hired (and paid for) by a person seeking a professional engagement as an employee or consultant.

Terminology	Definition
Experts	People who add measurable value with regards to subjects of interest to specific industry experience.
Failing Forward (Idea and book by John Maxwell)	This book teaches how to embrace failure and see it as part of the process of life long learning.
Gatekeeper	A person who influences the Decision Maker as they often are important to factor into the approach to the Decision Maker, they often hold an important relationship of confidence with the Decision Maker.
GlassDoor	An online tool that provides reviews of corporate culture by those that have worked at businesses reviewed. It also provides salary ranges.
Go-Giver (Idea and book by John David Mann and Bob Burg)	Describes the value of being a connector and a servant to others. It provides a clear mindset and process by which to engage to become a true blessing to others.
Good Footprint	The act of very intentional written or oral communication. It results in a digital "good footprint" within an organization that becomes a permanent reference point for qualifications and candidacy.
Head Hunter/Executive Recruiter	A person who is "retained" to introduce candidates to a company for a professional hire.
Human Brand	What emotions or notions people have of when your name comes up.
Indirect to Companies	When a person goes "indirect to companies" they are appealing to people who have an affiliation or relationship with a targeted company or individual but are outside a direct link to the company being targeted. For example, if I am targeting company Y, I may go to their banker or attorney who has a direct relationship, which becomes a potential "point of entry" to company Y.
Industry Expert	Someone with professional qualifications that enable them to render opinions worthy of "professional consideration" from others within the industry they are associated with.

Terminology	Definition
Industry Periodical	These are industry-specific resources that are often in hard copy (books) at libraries or available online at websites. Librarians are familiar with these resources list out valuable information about industries, key trends within the industries, or key players within the industries.
Intrapreneurship	The mindset of "thinking like an entrepreneur" or acting like an entrepreneur, done while holding a role in a traditional corporation.
Job Board	An online resource often claiming to have true "jobs" when it functions as a "lead source" to sell educational services, insurance, or other multi-level pitches. It's estimated up to 90% of these "jobs" do not exist.
Job Posting	A physical or digital description of job availability.
Job Versus Opportunity	A job is something that you do for the sole reason of a "paycheck." An opportunity is something that you do because it excites you and appeals to your sense of life purpose.
Lifestyle/Lifeskill	A lifestyle is how you live your life, or choices you make to pursue that life. A lifeskill is a valuable skill that you have learned or acquired over time to assure that you can pursue a lifestyle of your choice.
LinkedIn	An online tool designed to help you research, display skills, position value, identify, create, and nurture relationships.
Meaningless Documentation	Resumes or any generic document you might use in the employment pursuit is essentially meaningless as it does not speak to how you would do the work required and do it profitably for the organization. Every document in the exploration process needs to be customized to address the unique circumstances or requirements associated with the opportunity being explored. Meaningless documentation will achieve nothing other than you being treated as a Desperate Jobseeker.
Mentor	Someone who shares information or insight with you voluntarily. They may meet with you regularly or occasionally. They offer wisdom, insights, advice, and knowledge.

Terminology	Definition
Money (anything you can use to solve a problem for someone else)	A key philosophy of The Economy of One is that money is anything we can use to solve a problem for someone else. We believe people are very talented and skilled and that when investing these skills and talents in others we move the collective economy forward, as well as our individual economies as well. We believe that as you build a reputation as someone who adds value, you will be sought out by others who need this value. This philosophy in action opens the doors for a lifetime of tremendous opportunity and provides extraordinary opportunity to help your community, non-profits, entrepreneurs, businesses, and others.
Negotiating	The act of each party asking for what it wants. The goal of every negotiation is that each party feels satisfied that its basic terms and needs have been achieved throughout the negotiation process.
Networks vs. Relationships	People often confuse a large "network" of people with real "relationships." Networks are impersonal groups of people you randomly associate with (think of Facebook). Relationships are different. Relationships are an intentional effort with individuals who you purposely go out of your way to serve and get to know. How? By asking about their needs. You actively engage with them to help support them professionally in the marketplace and serve their families personally.
Offer	The written or oral details describing compensation associated with a professional role.
Offer Structure	The complete package of benefits, salary, and perks associated with the role. It includes things such as exit clauses, non-compete agreements, or any other negotiable component associated with the offer.
Onboarding	Once an offer to hire is extended and accepted, onboarding addresses the processes necessary to ensure engagement. This may include filling out necessary HR documentation, orientation, issuing a PO, or finalizing the details of an employment contract once a general agreement is obtained.

Terminology	Definition
Passion	An often overlooked ingredient to meaningful employment, entrepreneurial endeavors, or a well-lived life. Passion can be what drives you personally or professionally or can be the purpose of your life experience. As Dr. Denis Waitley says, "Begin each day with the end in mind."
Paycheck	A physical representation of why we might work, but it can be misleading as often the total value of a paycheck is not anywhere near the psychological toll it demands (you hate your "job"). Ideally, a paycheck is a representative of financial return on a true opportunity enjoyed and well done.
People Doing What You Want To Do	These are people who hold titles or roles within companies that align with what you ultimately desire to do (Story of You). Target them to establish a relationship, understand how they landed the role, and ask them for help in expanding your relationship base with recruiters or others in their industry with influence.
Personal Opportunity	An opportunity that excites you personally. This is something that makes sense for you and yours, whether it has anything to do with earning income or not. It is something that interests you, captivates your imagination, and is something you desire to explore.
Positioning	The act of intentionally describing and/or demonstrating the measurable corporate value or impact associated with your skills.
Professional Market Researcher	A person who has skills critical to conducting market research or the gathering of intelligence of all kinds. They may have an advanced degree such as an MBA or Ph.D., or if doing contract or "gig" work, maybe an undergraduate who happens to be very good at market research.
Professional Opportunity	An opportunity that excites you professionally. A true opportunity aligns with your passions and proficiencies, it is a match culturally for you and is a fit for your family.
Prospector	The entrepreneurial mindset and behaviors required to generate interest in skills or capabilities resulting in revenue.

Terminology	Definition
Qualifying An Opportunity	The intentional act of slowing down in the sales process to ask critical questions. To qualify means that you are engaged in the process of actively confirming details, positioning your unique value proposition with the customer's needs or details critical to the job/consulting opportunity.
Recruiter	A person that is paid on a "contingency" basis to introduce candidates to a company for professional hire.
Referral	The kind act of intentionally providing a resource, professional, or a personal recommendation to another.
Research Librarian	Professional researchers who work at libraries, they serve the general public. You can ask them for free help with questions you have on industries or individuals you are researching.
Resigning	The act of officially stepping down or out of a professional role. Often a letter of resignation is provided to officially begin the act of resignation.
Return On Investment	When businesses make a hire, either for a job or a contract, they look to solve a problem or create a value/profit that is more than the cost. This "excess value" is called a return on the initial investment. When people hire an individual, your pay and training represent the employer's or customer's investment. The employer or customer is always looking to make a return on that investment.
Revenue	Revenue is the total amount of income generated by the sale of goods or services related to the company's primary operations.
Story of You	This story is a summary of the value that you deliver to others. It explains why you are a unique solution that delivers measurable results to others. It speaks to the type of culture you work well with and the type of problems you solve or the way you add measurable value to those you associate with. It often addresses something that makes you vulnerable or "authentic." It explains why you are passionate, deeply motivated, or a unique solution, and this story might slightly change depending on whom it is being presented.
Technical Expert	The entrepreneurial mindset and behavior required by an individual to describe the technical qualifications, value, and scope of skills or work required when meeting with a potential buyer of such skills.

Terminology	Definition
Thank-You Note On Steroids	This is a deeply personalized thank-you note that details the exact next steps and often includes further documentation (amendment documents) that illustrate in detail the value you will create for a prospective employer or consulting client. It explains how you will do what needs to be done and do it profitably.
The Battlefield of the Mind (Joyce Meyer)	This book directly addresses the sources of fear, uncertainty, and doubt in our lives. It provides Biblical explanations on how to overcome each issue, moving forward.
The Scale of Value to Business Owners	A descriptive term that describes how valuable any proposition or skill might be to a business owner. What you might be offering may be very valuable to one particular business owner, or of little value to another owner. Your offering of skills and talents is unique to each situation and the associated needs of the business owner or potential buyer of your value.
Thought Leader	People who are considered "experts" within an industry. They participate in industry conferences, on expert panels, or write articles or blogs on industry developments. They are often sources of industry insights, trends, or analysis.
Traditional HR Process	A series of corporately defined processes that often are driven by technologies that too often depersonalize, complicate, and confuse the process. These processes are established to protect the corporation from liability, not necessarily attract the ideal candidate.
Trust	A critical factor required by our economy. Trust always is required before the transaction. Trust building behavior should be the ultimate goal of anyone seeking to become an Economy of One.
Two Things All People Love To Do	Talk about themselves and teach.
Up Front "Sales" Talk	A personal disclosure provided at the beginning of initial discussions, permitting each party to "exit " if there is no fit. It politely allows both parties to indicate early in the dialog if there is no fit or proper way forward.
Value Proposition	This is what you do or can do that uniquely adds measurable value or makes a measurable difference within a business context.

Terminology	**Definition**
War Room Strategy	A term used to describe a meeting designed to identify assumptions held by each party about the job or project at hand. The meeting will address assumptions each party has about timelines for the work to be done, strategies to be employed, processes to be followed, management expectations, assumptions about budget and resources available, as well as "definitions of success" for each party. The meeting is meant to confirm and solidify any last-minute understandings critical for both parties to determine that the engagement is a "good fit."
Warehouse of Skills	It is estimated each person has between 500-700 skills. These are all the things you can do personally or professionally to add value in any situation. The "warehouse" refers to the broad skills that you can access as circumstances demand.
X-Factor	The mysterious "can't be taught" characteristic people have with others or on their own. It enables them to make progress or find favor with others.

FAQs

I feel overwhelmed. How do I start my MAP?

Start by assembling a list of everyone you know: family, friends and acquaintances. Work from a spreadsheet if you can. It's much easier to track things like MAP ratings and meeting notes on a spreadsheet than on a simple list, although either will work. (Hint: Don't just assume all your contacts are in your Outlook or on your social media friend lists. Whole categories of contacts—like former professors, for example—are likely not on those lists.) Next, add contacts you wish you knew. Include people you want to know, whether individuals or companies or industries you want to focus on.

When you properly develop and attend to your MAP, it will guide your prospecting efforts. You'll know who to talk to—and when—in order to build a lifelong professional network and effective stream of opportunities.

Why do I need a YBR spreadsheet?   Can't I just use my MAP?

No, you need both tools to effectively run the THE ECONOMY OF ONE method. It's not just about managing relationships; it's about winning contracts. The YBR is a color-coded spreadsheet and a separate tool to help you immediately assess your weekly progress and set priorities. Your MAP, on the other hand, is a comprehensive list of contact names, like a customized phone book of all the people you could call on or appeal to for help.

Why use color codes?

Research suggests adult learners improve their retention by as much as 80% when something is color-coded. By color-coding the opportunities in your YBR pipeline, you will have a greater feel for how you are progressing and be more able to communicate to others your current status and priorities. With one glance at the colors in your pipeline, you'll know how you're doing.

What's a Yellow, Blue or Red? Is it the opportunity, a contact in a company or the company itself?

The colors refer to the opportunities themselves. However, each opportunity has a contact associated with it—a White (so called because contacts are blank slates who could lead you anywhere).

When I first create my YBR, are there issues I should be aware of?

Sometimes, when people do a first draft of their YBR, they mislabel the opportunities in the pipeline. That causes them to misinterpret the data and get confused about what to do next with each opportunity. Make sure you really understand the color definitions and be very careful to apply the color codes properly.

How should I interpret my YBR? What should I look for?

When someone starts the program, rarely do they have a healthy spread of Yellow, Blue, Red in the pipeline. (A healthy spread is six yellows to every two blues to every one red, or 6:2:1). Rather, you might see this: too many Yellows, too few Blues, or confusing Reds that are unclear in terms of what "next steps" to take to reach post-sales.

Too Many Yellows—If this is your struggle, then chances are you are an outgoing person who connects with many people and may be tracking too many things. How are you meeting the challenge to follow up on all those known opportunities? Be careful not to keep adding Yellows without paying proper attention to the ones already in your pipeline.

Too Few Blues—A "Blue hole" in your pipeline is a common challenge. If there are too few Blues, it means you are either struggling to convert Yellows to Blue, or, you're rushing things to Red too fast.

No Reds—Do not panic. It sometimes takes a while to work the process long enough to be in a closing stage. Recognize that sales is a process; it has definitive time frames, and your best effort is spent doing what you can with where you are. Things do move forward in time. Keep working to qualify Blues so you can convert them to Reds.

Many Lost Reds—This suggests that you may be interviewing for the wrong types of positions or that you could use additional coaching on how to close.

I hate sales. I've never been in sales. Why in the world do I need to approach my search like this?

Whether you ever realize it or not, you are in a sales position if you are looking for work of any type. In effect, you are in the position of having to sell yourself and your abilities. Start by shifting the way you see yourself: You are more than simply a teacher, an engineer, a plumber, or marketing executive. Armed with your skillset and experience (as the Technical Expert), aim to market yourself as a Prospector, and to secure your next opportunity as a Closer. Selling is a role-specific process, and it takes some practice (and a change in mindset) to get comfortable with it, no matter what your skillset may be, or whether you are an introvert or an extrovert.

What are the bottom-line definitions of White, Yellow, Blue, Red, and Green?

White is a person or company you want to focus on and communicate with to discuss your capabilities. Whites are not opportunities. They are contacts or connections that may lead to opportunities.

Yellow is a confirmed opportunity. A conversation (with a real person) has led you to confirm a real opportunity exists and you can take action on it.

Blue is a confirmed opportunity that has moved now to a different stage, where a contact (or prospect) has asked for a meeting to discuss a specific opportunity. In other words, there is enough urgency related to the opportunity that the prospect is willing to take a meeting to discuss it.

Red is a confirmed opportunity that has progressed even further. You've answered the Eight Critical Questions. Now, you and the prospect are in final negotiations in an attempt to close the deal, one way or the other.

Green is any opportunity that has reached a final resolution – either awarded or denied.

How should I use THE ECONOMY OF ONE to help me with time management?

THE ECONOMY OF ONE is very helpful in determining whether you are making tangible progress in the way you are spending your time. I encourage people to post a paycheck amount – representing what they made in a past job, or projecting what they would like to earn in a future one – near a computer, on a bathroom mirror, or on the refrigerator to remind them of the value of their time. When one participant did this, she realized she needed to make much better use of her time. For every TV show she watched, every nap she took, and every time she engaged in web surfing, it was costing her, on average, $18/hour based on her former wage.

You can gauge what your time is worth by continually evaluating and updating your YBR. The outcomes are associated with the way you invest your time. Remember, once you invest an hour, you cannot get it back. THE ECONOMY OF ONE helps you become more focused and intentional with how you use your time, because you constantly see the real results of how you spend it.

Should I keep a weekly scorecard of my progress?

Absolutely. It is helpful to keep clear goals to stay motivated and to remind yourself that, no matter how things feel, you are making progress. Typical weekly goals include three new Yellows, one Blue, or one Red.

What's the best way to ask others for help?

Asking for help is the most difficult step to take for many people, but it is often the most important one. Look to identify other people in similar situations to share leads and information—through your own network, of course, but also through workshops, job fairs, online forums, and even volunteering. Do not neglect to position yourself as a good source of information to others in the same boat, because a good deed often leads to an even better one in return.

When working through THE ECONOMY OF ONE, take the time to figure out what you really want (your perfect job, your personal brand, etc.). You must drill down to what you really want to do so you can clearly articulate to others *how* they can help you. The more you can define your direction, the more you will be able to maximize your ability to get to the right decision makers and identify opportunities before they become public knowledge.

How much time should I really spend volunteering?

You are encouraged to invest 30% of whatever time you have available volunteering. Ideally, you should seek out those places where you can offer your professional skills. Volunteering provides opportunities on so many levels. For example, the chance to be productive while giving back, which will fill you up at a time when you are likely feeling lost or empty. It also helps expand your contacts, skills and experience. And of course, there is so much of a need out there for volunteers with various levels of expertise. It is a significant win-win for all.

My situation seems hopeless as my unemployment has stretched far beyond what I expected.

You are not alone in this and I can sympathize. While it may seem hopeless, this could be the time for you to identify other options. If whatever you have been doing is not working, it's time to consider doing something else, or to find another approach. This is what working with THE ECONOMY OF ONE is all about: systematically approaching your dilemma from a very different angle! As I spend time visiting with job, and life coaches, community leaders, and others whose primary focus is on unemployment issues, what is very clear is that our current system for helping people find jobs is not adequate.

According to the Wall Street Journal, one in four people (and this number is expected to grow over time) are not ever going back to Corporate America in a full-time capacity. At best, the WSJ suggests those workers will shift from working as full-time employees to working as contractors, having to "re-sell" their capabilities every 12-24 months. Give yourself permission to try a fresh approach and explore other paths you have not considered before now. It's time to think out-of-the-box. THE ECONOMY OF ONE is the way.

A great reading resource I highly recommend is Battlefield of the Mind by Joyce Meyer. It is a best-selling book that squarely addresses the voices of fear, uncertainty, and doubt during times like these. Another great resource is DrLynnJoseph.com. Her CDs have been statistically shown to multiply by six your odds of finding employment.

I think I may be suffering from post-traumatic interview disorder. I feel burned out. Where can I get help?

Give yourself some mental time off. Take time to work out, be in nature, listen to music, meditate, reach out to friends, or ask for prayer if you belong to any kind of faith community. Be gentle with yourself and know, "This too shall pass."

Should you encounter rejection repeatedly, it is normal to have your confidence shaken, and for doubt to cloud your mind. But if you feel particularly weighed down by this, address your concerns with your accountability partner, as well as with a doctor, professional or spiritual advisor to help anchor you. Self-care during this process is absolutely essential.

I want to sleep all the time and am having a hard time engaging. What do I do?

Consider making an appointment to see your doctor to make sure there is not a physical problem. Once this is eliminated, you might be suffering from a clinical depression. If this is the case, get professional help or counseling. If you do not have a doctor, or cannot afford medical care, get to a church or other spiritual resource where you can talk to someone about how to deal with your depression; join a small prayer or support group. Or, join an online forum at EconomyOfOne.com

You are not alone. Depression is a serious condition. Seek help anywhere you can find it.

How long do I maintain my MAP?

Update your MAP as regularly as possible, whether you have a job, are looking for one, or not. In other words, for the length of your career. Find a rhythm or system that works for you whether you update or check it on a weekly or monthly basis – for instance, when you pay your bills. You could find your circumstances might unexpectedly change at any time; keep your MAP current, and all the vital information in it will be at your fingertips when you need it most.

Is there a CODE course or book designed specifically for businesses or entrepreneurs?

Yes. *Driving Demand* is available on Amazon.com.

I am not in sales (and do not plan to be) but wondered if there was an actual process salespeople typically follow?

Yes. If you are interested, here is a typical approach to sales:
A sales rep identifies a potential opportunity (this is known as lead generation). The sales rep confirms a potential customer needs a product/service and has a budget and a timeline for a decision to be made (this is known as the initial lead qualification). The sales rep gathers more information and asks questions to determine the urgency and sensitivity to price versus perception of value (this is another lead qualification step). A technician reviews the scope of the transaction requirements (this is yet another lead qualification step). The technician creates a project proposal (this is preparing for the sales pitch). The technician sends the proposal to his or her manager (continuing to prepare for the sales pitch). The manager reviews the proposal and approves (or disapproves) the approach and price (leading up to the actual pitch). The sales rep presents the general parameters of the deal to the prospect, makes adjustments, and re-submits the adjusted proposal to the manager or closer (this is a sales pitch moving to a close). The manager/closer presents the final price to the potential customer or prospect and makes the push to finalize negotiation and deal (the sales pitch moving to a close). The customer or prospect reviews the final proposal, and decides it is a go or no-go (moving the project to the post-sales phase). The sales rep asks for a referral and the cycle repeats.

The Four Phases in Making a Sale:

These phases are what all companies engage in all the time whether they recognize it or not.

- Opportunity Generation—where you identify potential jobs or contracts, and generate interest in your ability to fulfill the needs of the job or contract
- Opportunity Qualification—where you evaluate the opportunities or contracts you've found
- The Sales Pitch—where you work towards an agreement for the position
- Post-Sales—where you engage in the tasks that follow a yes or no from the negotiations

Made in the USA
Monee, IL
18 April 2024

57061641R00090